# Quips, Quotes and Savvy Sayings

# Also by Phyllis Martin

*Word Watcher's Handbook: A Deletionary of the Most Abused and Misused Words*

*Martin's Magic Formula for Getting the Right Job*

*Martin's Magic Motivation Book: How to Become an Anointed One in Your Organization*

*Return To Chipping Sodbury*

*Killing Is Murder* (pseudonym Pleiades)

### Children's Books

*Turn On the Dark*

*A Moving Time for Kelly*

*A New Blanket for Josh*

*Katie's Mild Animal Hunt*

# Quips, Quotes and Savvy Sayings

## A Resource for Lovers of the Language

*Phyllis Martin*

iUniverse, Inc.
New York  Lincoln  Shanghai

Quips, Quotes and Savvy Sayings
A Resource for Lovers of the Language

Copyright © 2006 by Phyllis R. Martin

All rights reserved. No part of this book may be used or reproduced by any means, graphic, electronic, or mechanical, including photocopying, recording, taping or by any information storage retrieval system without the written permission of the publisher except in the case of brief quotations embodied in critical articles and reviews.

iUniverse books may be ordered through booksellers or by contacting:

iUniverse
2021 Pine Lake Road, Suite 100
Lincoln, NE 68512
www.iuniverse.com
1-800-Authors (1-800-288-4677)

ISBN-13: 978-0-595-38859-2 (pbk)
ISBN-13: 978-0-595-83238-5 (ebk)
ISBN-10: 0-595-38859-0 (pbk)
ISBN-10: 0-595-83238-5 (ebk)

Printed in the United States of America

# ACKNOWLEDGMENTS

Marian Charrier, bridge authority and my esteemed instructor, deserves thanks. Without Marian's prodding, I would never have embarked upon the screamingly hard task of developing order from the chaos my huge stash of notes represented.

I also acknowledge long-treasured gifts of children's sayings from Pat Diehl and Terri Byczkowski, as well as those from a few others whose names have disappeared from the gifts. You probably know who you are. Hope so.

Then too, I'm grateful for help and suggestions from friends Nancy Walker, Wolf Eschenlohr, Marion Glaser, Eileen Hiles, Millie Rath, Camille Mercer, and Mary A. White.

I owe special thanks to Emilie Jacobson for her thoughtful critique of an early draft of this book.

Finally, and always, to husband Bruce. Bruce is a writer and dedicated typochondriac. He admits to editing and proof-reading this book.

# CONTENTS

ACKNOWLEDGMENTS ..................................................................v

INTRODUCTION ........................................................................ix

PART I ............................................................................................1
    WORDS ABOUT WORDS FOR SMARTIES ..............................3
        Quips, Quotes and Savvy Sayings about Words

PART II ..........................................................................................7
    WORDS ABOUT WORK FOR SMARTIES ................................9
        Quips, Quotes and Savvy Sayings about Work

PART III ......................................................................................15
    SMARTIES ARE SUPERB COMMUNICATORS ....................17
        They:  A. Ask for help.
                 B. Benefit from the Terrible Ten.
                 C. Use the Conversational Pie.
                 D. Discover additional errors via a word test.
                 E. Eliminate tired words and phrases.
                 F. Flag down the watch words.
                 G. Use the correct abbreviations for state names.

PART IV ......................................................................................39
    AS THE WORLD TERMS ........................................................41
        Quips, Quotes and Savvy Sayings about
        the Way the World Wags

## PART V ............................................................................51
### TERMS TO TEMPT THE CREATIVE COMMUNICATOR
#### EPONYMS—NAMES THAT BECAME WORDS ...............53
#### ANIMAL TALK ..................................................................64
#### SMALL TALK ....................................................................70

## PART VI ...........................................................................77
### WORDS OF FAREWELL ...........................................................79

## THE LAST WORD ...............................................................87
## BIBLIOGRAPHY ..................................................................89
## INDEX ................................................................................91

# INTRODUCTION

Many writers tell you they had mentors who encouraged them to write their books. My experience is different. I had a tormentor, Marian Charrier. Marian insisted that I put what she terms "your sayings" in book form for others to enjoy. At first my response was a loud and discourteous "**No**." But then, after several sessions of office clean-up, I realized I had filled several notebooks with quips, quotes and savvy sayings that should be passed along. Let them form grooves in someone else's brain, I figured.

This book is not another offering for "Dummies." It's for you smart ones who have an insatiable love of our language and welcome any enhancer that gives it flavor.

So here you are. I hope each dollop packs a wallop that serves to ignite your teachings, preachings, or speeches and even serves to make your ordinary conversation less ordinary.

# PART I

Words about Words for Smarties
    Quips, Quotes and Savvy Sayings about Words

# WORDS ABOUT WORDS FOR SMARTIES

This portion of the book comes from my reservoir of quotes, quips and sayings about the importance of words. Their purpose is to enliven speeches and writings. I haven't actually plagiarized any of the gems you see here. Rather, I've called attention to the good writing of others. Where possible, I've named them.

Let's start with my all-time favorite quote about words, Proverbs 25:11—"A word fitly spoken is like apples of gold in settings of silver."

From Oliver Wendell Holmes we have these gems: "All of a person's antecedents are summed up in a single utterance, which gives at once the gauge of a person's education and mental organization."

and

"A word is not a crystal, transparent and unchanging. It is the skin of a living thought and may vary in color and content according to the circumstances and the time in which it is used."

Ronald Geller said, "Words are the clothes the mind wears."

Mark Twain said, "A powerful agent is the right word."

According to Ernest Weekley, "Stability in language is synonymous with rigor mortis."

President Gerald R. Ford said: "If I went back to college again, I'd concentrate on two areas: learning to write and to speak before an audience. Nothing in life is more important than the ability to communicate effectively."

Paul Tillich said, "Language has created the word loneliness to express the pain of being alone and the word solitude to express the glory of being alone."

According to Edwin H. Land, "The world belongs to the articulate."

C.S. Lewis made this observation about writing: "I sometimes think that writing is like driving sheep down a road. If there is any gate to the left or right, the reader will most certainly go for it."

"A sentence should read as if the author, had he held a plow instead of a pen, could have drawn a furrow deep and straight to the end."—Henry Thoreau

The late Leo Hirtl, Managing Editor of *The Cincinnati Post*, said: "Remember that famous memo from Moses. You were riveted by the short imperative sentences such as 'Thou shalt not steal,' 'Thou shalt not commit adultery.' Make your sentences brief (and he shouted this part), **Long sentences are for criminals."**

According to George Santayana, brevity is "almost a condition of being inspired."

I believe I received this gem from The Association for Women in Communications. "The strongest drive is not love or hate. It is one person's need to ~~change~~ alter another's copy."

Words are the tools of the brain. When you blunt them, you blunt your message.

From Caleb C. Colton we have this: "Words are but the signs and counters of knowledge, and their currency should be strictly regulated by the capital which they represent."

Ralph Waldo Emerson offered this advice: "No man has a prosperity so high or firm, but that two or three words can dishearten it; and there is no calamity which right words will not begin to redress."

Mr. Emerson also said: "A man cannot speak but he judges and reveals himself. With his will, or against his will, he draws his portrait to the eyes of others by every word."

A Japanese proverb reveals this truth: "One kind word can warm three winter months."

"A good word is an easy obligation; but not to speak ill requires only our silence, which costs us nothing."—Tillotson.

"The pen is mightier than the sword."—Edward Bulwer-Lytton.

This version of the message may be old but it has more punch than "The word processor is mightier than the bomb."

Speaking of pens, John Greenleaf Whittier was on target with this message:

> "For all the words of tongue or pen,
>
> The saddest are these: 'It might have been'!"

John Wilson said, "The knowledge of words is the gate of scholarship."

From an Ann Landers column: "The weaker the ideas, the stronger the language. A person whose thinking lacks substance often laces it with profanity in an effort to give it muscle. In a word—he's intellectually bankrupt."

"You erect a sound barrier between you and your listener when you misuse words," maintains Julie Simpson.

From Frederika Bremer: "There are words which sever hearts more than sharp swords; there are words the point of which sting the heart through the course of life."

Abd-el-Kader said, "It is with a word as with an arrow—once let it loose and it does not return."

Isn't it great to live in a country where you can say what you think without thinking?

From John Caspar Lavater: "Learn the value of a man's words and expressions, and you know him. He who has a superlative for everything wants a measure for the great or small."

Shakespeare told us: "When words are scarce they're seldom spent in vain."

"You're only as good as your word."

"It is important to express for success as well as to dress for success."

"Create professionalism with your voice."

If you use quotations, try to get them right. Examples: It is "Music hath charms to soothe the savage breast" (not beast). And, "Not all that tempts your wand'ring eyes and heedless hearts, is lawful prize; Nor all, that glisters gold." No, it is not glistens here.

Byron got it right. He wrote, "But Shakespeare also says, "...To gild fine gold, or paint the lily." (How many times have you heard someone say, "To gild the lily"?)

Rochefoucauld made this observation: "The reason so few people are agreeable in conversation is that each is thinking more about what he intends to say than about what others are saying, and we never listen when we are eager to speak."

"The real art of conversation is not only to say the right thing at the right time, but also to leave unsaid the wrong thing at the tempting moment."

"There are many great opportunities for you to keep your mouth shut. Don't miss them."

I close this segment with my second-most favorite quotation. It is from Psalms 141:3. "Set a guard over my mouth, O Lord, keep watch over the door of my lips!"

# PART II

Words about Work for Smarties
   Quips, Quotes and Savvy Sayings about Work

# WORDS ABOUT WORK FOR SMARTIES

Ever since human resources was called "personnel" I've been savoring these true gems. Here you have not merely the most thought-provoking; you have the most useful. All right, some are included for humor.

The boss values **appearance** and the more regular the better.

In **brainstorming** the ideas you didn't present can prove to be the best of all.

Byron told us, "The **busy** have no time for tears."

Take time to **carve a career:** it beats chiseling.

**Change** is the most constant thing we have; learn to channel it. To fight change is to lose. To be passive is at best a tie. To accept the challenge of change, to actually help shape the future, is to win. The only human beings who actually welcome a change are wet babies.

Show **confidence**—Don't worry about a little trembling. When you vibrate it means you're alive.

Tell yourself this: I work for myself and I believe in the product.

You are your major resource.

If we talked to others as we do to ourselves we wouldn't have any friends.

Learn to speak for yourself. If you don't speak, even God can't hear you.

A **consultant** is part of the advice squad.

Show **creativity**—A culinary arts grad took two dinners to his interview. Yes, he was hired—both for his creativity and for his culinary ability. Here's more food for thought: If a VIP, boss, or prospective employer invites you to dine, select food that's easy to eat.

Jerome Klapka Jerome had some priceless comments about the enjoyment of **work**. He said "It is impossible to enjoy idling thoroughly unless one has plenty of work to do." He also said, "I like work; it fascinates me. I can sit and look at it for hours. I love to keep it by me; the idea of getting rid of it nearly breaks my heart."

About **failure**—Henry Ford said that "failure is only the opportunity to begin again more intelligently."

Expect the best but prepare for the worst.

Rejection should not engender rage but re-assessment.

Failure is the line of least persistence.

"Show me a thoroughly satisfied man—and I will show you a failure."—Thomas A. Edison

Thomas Watson said, "The way to succeed is to double your failure rate."

If the mind sees failure, the body goes along.

The winner is always part of the answer, the loser always part of the problem.

The winner always has a plan; the loser always has an excuse.

Don't pave a rut.

Will Rogers warned us about ruts. He said, "Even if you're on the right track, you'll get run over if you just sit there."

Danny Thomas gave this advice, "Thoroughbreds don't look at other horses. They wear blinders and run their own race."

**Fame**—"Fame is proof that people are gullible."—Ralph Waldo Emerson

> Fame is the scentless sunflower,
>
> With gaudy crown of gold;
>
> But friendship is the breathing rose,
>
> With sweets in every fold.
>
> Oliver Wendell Holmes

**Friends**—"A friendship based on business is better than a business founded on friendship," according to John D. Rockefeller, Jr.

When you service all of people's needs they won't come back, but their friends will.

**Future**—What you are to be you are now becoming.

It's possible to create the future you want.

A **goal** without a plan is only a wish.

Examine your soul as well as your goal.

Goals are dreams written down, and those dreams have deadlines.

People without goals are used by people with them.

**Idea**—The birth of a notion.

**Luck** is looking for a needle in a haystack and coming out with the farmer's daughter.

Anatole France told us, "Chance is the pseudonym God uses when he doesn't want to sign his name."

When preparation and opportunity meet it's called luck. Serendipity is latching on to luck.

Jim Blasingame, The Small Business Advocate, said, "Expect serendipity whenever you risk what you know for what you might learn."

The weak hope for something to happen. The strong make it happen.

"Luck is an accident that happens to the competent."—Albert M. Greenfield

**Money**—"The darkest hour in any person's life is when he sits down to plan how to get money without earning it," warned Horace Greeley.

**Nepotism**—Hire your parents, your children, your siblings. Remember nepotism is only kin deep.

**Persistence**—Calvin Coolidge maintained that "Nothing in the world can take the place of persistence. *Talent* will not; nothing is more common than unsuccessful people with talent. *Genius* will not; unrewarded genius is almost a proverb. *Education* will not; the world is full of educated derelicts. Persistence alone is omnipotent."

**Quality**—When the product doesn't come back but the customer does.

**Risk**—"Not to take risks is the biggest risk," according to Roberto Goizueta.

Be willing to take reasonable risks. As Barbara Proctor says, "If you make only right turns, you'll be going in circles."

**Sales savvy**—If you're selling hand organs don't talk to the monkey.

Make contacts if you want to make contracts.

Ask for the order. Most people have trouble making up their minds. Help them.

You can't sell from an empty wagon.

From Proverbs 22:1 we learn this: "Goodwill, like a good name, is won by many acts and lost by one."

Talk about benefits before you talk price. Remington took out an ad saying you could get 13 shavers for the price of one Remington and then explained the benefits of Remington's product before he named Remington's price.

**Success**—Woody Allen says, "Ninety percent of success is just showing up."

Success is relative. The more success the more relatives.

Success comes in cans. Failure comes in can'ts.

The elevator to success could be out of order; you may have to take the stairs.

Zig Ziglar said "I've met a lot of people who won't make it but none who can't."

According to David Brinkley, "A successful person can build a solid foundation with the bricks others have thrown at him."

Barry Switzer was quoted in the Kansas City *Times* as saying, "Some people are born on third base and go through life thinking they hit a triple."

Learn to swim with sharks but don't let them see you bleed.

You won't be successful until you have a stronger desire to get things done than to be liked.

The winner sees an answer for every problem; the loser sees a problem in every answer.

In my talk "How to be a Bone-afide Success," I said you had to have good bone structure to get ahead at work: a back bone (sticking to the job), a wish bone (setting goals), a jaw bone (improving what comes out of your month) and a funny bone (learning to take yourself lightly and your job seriously).

Expect bruised shins as you climb the ladder of success.

Renowned communications expert Sonya Hamlin said, "If you want a place in the sun, you must be prepared to get a few blisters."

If you wish to appear on top of your job, promise everything later than it can be delivered.

Be sure you're underpaid; that is, make certain that your contributions are worth more than the money you receive.

**Tenacity**—Old age and treachery can overcome youth and skill.

**Time**—Carl Sandburg said, "Time is the coin of your life. It is the only coin you have, and only you can determine how it will be spent. Be careful lest you let other people spend it for you."

If you don't have the time to take a bore to dinner, send him one.

There is all the time in the world. There always is, if you let there be.

**Training**—If you think training is expensive, you ought to try ignorance.

If you don't want to get the wrong kind of job, you'll need to get the right kind of training.

It's not what you don't know that hurts you. It's what you think you know that isn't so.

Let's let Jacob Neusner have the final say for this segment: "If I teach you how to work, to have good attitudes, to take responsibility for your own ideas, to communicate and to think a problem through, no matter what subject matter I use in order to get those basic skills of mind and intellect across, then I'm giving you something you can use for a very long time. Those skills will never change."

# PART III

Smarties Are Superb Commumicators
- They:
  - A. Ask for help.
  - B. Benefit from the Terrible Ten.
  - C. Use the Conversational Pie.
  - D. Discover additional errors via a word test.
  - E. Eliminate tired words and phrases.
  - F. Flag down the watch words.
  - G. Use the correct abbreviations for state names.

# SMARTIES ARE SUPERB COMMUNICATORS

It's great to be entertaining with words but we can also use words to enlighten. The truly vibrant speaker offers a substantive message but doesn't jar the listener with misused words while doing it.

Would you like to become a truly superb communicator? It's easy as ABCDEFG.

A. Ask someone around you—colleague, family member or friend—to tell you about any abused or misused words in your vocabulary. Then, go on to ask if you're guilty of peppering your speech with tics and burrs that produce "hear-ache" in your listener's ear. Examples: you know, at any rate, and that, that's for sure, that sort of thing, like, basically, okay.

I can vouch for the effectiveness of this practice. Before submitting the manuscript for *Word Watcher's Handbook*, I asked my husband to tell me about any errors I might make. Get that might. What a shock to learn he had my list ready. "Why didn't you tell me?" I wailed. "Because you didn't ask," he replied.

Listen tight: here are a couple of my errors. I referred to "grammatical errors," when I should have said "errors in grammar." "Grammatical error" is an oxymoron. I also misused the word nauseous. I said two milk shakes would make me "nauseous" when I should have said two milk shakes would make me "nauseated." I assure you I can be nauseous, but that means I cause nausea.

Pay-back time finally arrived. I couldn't resist dedicating my writing, "To Bruce, who taught me the meaning of nauseous."

B. Benefit from the most frequently mentioned errors list I compiled from my book. I've dubbed the errors "THE TERRIBLE TEN."

## THE TERRIBLE TEN

1. Misuse of the word I. It is not "between you and I." It is between you and **me**. It is not, "She sent the report to Steve and I." **Correct:** "She sent the report to Steve and **me**." One can test oneself by dropping the name of the other person, in this case Steve. Would you say, "She sent the report to I"? Of course not.
2. "It don't" instead of it doesn't. It helps to remember that it don't is a shortened version of it do not (a phrase that would sound awkward to you).
3. "Can't hardly" instead of can hardly.
4. "Irregardless" instead of regardless.
5. A lot written as one word. **Correct:** a lot. **Incorrect:** "alot."
6. Use of an unnecessary S. Examples: "somewheres" instead of somewhere, "anywheres" instead of anywhere, "a ways" instead of a way (the a before way should signify that way is singular). Imagine, if you will, Judy Garland's singing, "Somewheres over the rainbow." Wouldn't that produce "hear-ache"?
7. "Heighth" instead of height. Notice that height ends in t, and you will pronounce it correctly.
8. "Youse" as a plural of you.
9. Incorrect use of the word myself. Do not say, "Myself and Bruce are going to town." **Correct:** "Bruce and I are going to town."
10. "You was" instead of you were. Or, similarly, "we done" instead of we did.

C. Look at the **Conversational Pie Chart** on the next page. If you would be a glistening conversationalist, learn to listen. Study the word glistening, and remind yourself that the biggest part of the word glistening is listening.

Conversation is but carving!
Give no more to every guest
Than he's able to digest.
Give him always of the prime,
And but a little at a time.
Carve to all but just enough,
Let them neither starve nor stuff,
And that you may have your due,
Let your neighbor carve for you.

                        Jonathan Swift

**CONVERSATIONAL PIES**

Your share when two of you are talking.

Your share when three of you are talking.

Your share when four of you are talking.

You in a crowd.

Reprinted from *Martin's Magic Motivation Book*

You can judge your listening by envisioning a conversational pie. If two of you are engaged in conversation, your share of talk time is roughly 50 percent. Notice how your share becomes smaller as the group becomes larger. Take more than your share only if urged.

Wilson Mizner describes a good listener as a person who "is not only popular everywhere, but after a while he knows something."

D. Discover any additional errors you might make by taking the word test. Admittedly, this test is a bit more difficult than the ones I typically use in my word clinic.

## HELP FOR HEAR-ACHE TEST

I promise: there is "help for hear-ache." In order to learn whether you're a pain in the ear, please answer these twenty questions. Give yourself five points for each correct answer. The bonus question is also worth five points and will serve to increase your score.

#1. A good writer is (persnickety or pernickety) about going over copy.

#2. I enjoy visiting The Smithsonian (Institution or Institute).

#3. I am (adverse or averse) to correcting other people's speech.

#4. The player was sidelined because he had a temperature. Anything wrong with that statement?

#5. The lawyer issued an affidavid. Is affidavid correct?

#6. After just one week in Hawaii, she was eager to be stateside again. Would this statement offend anyone?

#7. He only wished to run one marathon. Is this statement correct?

#8. James J. Kilpatrick is a man that has a superb writing style. Does this sentence sound all right to you?

#9. I put my notes on the podium so they would be within easy reach. Anything wrong with this statement?

#10. I sent a report in (regard, regards) to your complaint.

#11. I told her I trusted her to be (discrete or discreet).

#12. The minister asked us to study the Book of (Revelations or Revelation).

#13. He came to the Reds as the result of a fortuitous trade. Were we fans lucky?

#14. The Human Resources Association invited members of both the print and electronic media to a press conference. Why did so few representatives of the electronic media attend?

#15. Terri said, "I second the nomination." Can you spot an error here?

#16. He was proud to swear allegiance to the State of Kentucky. Can this statement be improved?

#17. They celebrated their 6-month anniversary. Is this statement correct?

#18. She was delighted to offer congratulations to the bride. Was the bride pleased to be congratulated?

#19. This is an amazing (phenomena or phenomenon).

#20. Citizens of Great Britain watch the activities of Prince Harry very carefully. Is this statement correct?

Bonus Question: If I say tennis is my forte, should I pronounce forte with one syllable or two?

Please score yourself.

#1. Pernickety is preferred. Do check the spelling of this word and you'll say it correctly.

#2. It is The Smithsonian Institution.

#3. The correct word is averse.

#4. The player was sidelined because his temperature was elevated. He had a fever.

#5. The lawyer may have been named David, but it was an affidavit that he issued. Affidavit ends in a t.

#6. Hawaii is a state. Hawaiians do not appreciate being excluded as they are when you say "stateside." Say *mainland* instead.

#7. As the sentence is written, it says all he did was wish. It should read: He wished to run only one marathon. James J. Kilpatrick says, "Misplacing one's 'only' is a crime against syntax."

#8. James J. Kilpatrick is a "man who" not a "man that." Note: I used all right correctly with this question.

#9. If I put my notes on the podium I'd have quite a reach, because one stands on the podium. The podium refers to a raised platform. The word podium has the same stem as that of podiatrist.

#10. The preferred word is regard. When you use regards, it sounds as though you are sending greetings.

#11. The word you wanted is discreet. Discreet means marked by exercising or showing prudence. Discrete refers to constituting a separate thing: distinct.

#12. I'll bet he asked you to study the Book of Revelation. The full name is the Revelation of St. John the Divine. (There is no s at the end of Revelation.) See Oscar Wilde's comment regarding life in the chapter on "How the World Terms." Yes, he does say Revelations, but he was using the word for humor in dialogue.

#13. In its best established sense fortuitous means "happening by accident or chance" with no implication as to the desirability of the outcome. H.W. Fowler labeled the use of fortuitous as a happy occurrence a malapropism. It is still widely regarded as incorrect. Communicators who are unwilling to risk censure are advised to avoid it.

#14. A press conference seems to limit the invitation to members of the print media. Representatives of the electronic media do not usually regard a "press conference" with favor. Try news conference if you wish to include everyone.

#15. It is not necessary for anyone to second a nomination. Furthermore, a moderator should not ask for a second to a nomination. The reason? It could cause unnecessary embarrassment if a second were not forthcoming.

#16. The official name for Kentucky is "The Commonwealth of Kentucky." Commonwealth is also used to refer to Pennsylvania, Massachusetts and Virginia. Puerto Rico is also considered a commonwealth.

#17. The word anniversary usually refers to an annual event. Study the Latin version of the word and you'll see why this is so. The picky, picky prefer to refer to a 6-month celebration.

#18. Those who are socially aware still insist that one offers best wishes to the bride while congratulating the bridegroom. Bridegroom is preferred over groom. A groom grooms horses. And no matter when or where you use the word congratulations please note that there are two t's in the word. It is not congradulations.

#19. Because you are talking about a one-time event, you should use the singular form of the word and refer to an amazing phenomenon. The superb communicator studies those Latin words such as alumnus (singular), alumni (plural), and datum (singular) and data (plural) and is cautious about their use.

#20. The sentence should refer to British subjects. Great Britain is a monarchy.

Bonus Question: Forte is pronounced with one syllable when referring to one's strong point. In music, it means strong or loud, and you pronounce it for-tay.

If you scored fewer than 70 points, you're jarring ear drums about 30 percent of the time. I urge you to get a copy of my *Word Watcher's Handbook, A Deletionary Of The Most Abused And Misused Words*.

Thanks to Ann Landers, who praised the book in her column, you can probably borrow a copy from your Public Library. The libraries ordered a ton of them. If you'd like to own a copy, you can order it from Amazon.com or through your favorite book store.

If you scored 100 or 105 points, I'll welcome your tips on how to improve my writing. Thanks.

E. Eliminate the phrases that are not so savvy.

## NOT SO SAVVY PHRASES

Without being crotchety about our quest for crisp language skills, it's wise to pause for a few minutes in order to determine what is not savvy. Here are phrases that are overdue for oblivion. You can do without most of these clichés and I earnestly hope you will.

active consideration
a dime a dozen
a drop in the bucket
aid and abet
armed to the teeth
at the crossroads—"The Crowded Crossroads," by J. Bruce Martin, Ph.D., in *The Journal of Irreproducible Results, 3$^{rd}$ Ed.*, cites 31 papers having the word crossroads in the title.
at the end of the day—This phrase is becoming threadbare when used to refer to "in conclusion."
back to the drawing board
beck and call
beyond the shadow of a doubt
bottom line
bound and determined
burn one's bridges
close but no cigar
conceptualize (How about envision instead?)
conspicuous by its absence
don't go there
feeding frenzy
flavor of the month
flip flop/flip flopping (as used politically)
front burner
get more bang for your buck
going forward
having a field day
here's the scenario

how fun
I approve this message
I get the picture
I hear what you're saying
it remains to be seen
I've got a bead on it
I want to thank…(Why not just thank the person instead of declaring an intention?)
knee-jerk reaction
light at the end of the tunnel
move into high gear
my bad
net-zero
no problem (If you are training servers, please teach them to say something similar to, "It would be a pleasure.")
no sweat
on the same page
picture of health (or death)
pillar of society
pockets of resistance
point in time
proud heritage
pursuit of excellence
put the pedal to the metal
right and proper
short shelf life (when it refers to something other than merchandise)
sum and substance
take with a grain of salt
tell it like it is
that's the ticket
the brass ring passes by but once
thinking outside the box—This phrase has become such a cliché that Kirk Cheyfitz turned the phrase inside out and made it the title of his provocative and readable book, *Thinking Inside the Box*.

tip of the iceberg
wait 'til next year—Cincinnati Reds' fans are particularly tired of this one.
walking encyclopedia
walking papers
wardrobe malfunction
wealth of information
whole new ballgame
you can say that again
you don't have to be a rocket scientist to…
you know what I'm saying?
you're fired

A cliché is not necessarily a poor way to say something. Quite the opposite. Phrases become clichés because they are so effective that they are over-used.

James J. Kilpatrick gives this reluctant warning: "Beware the old clichés. They have been ridden to death. Let us vow to ride some new clichés instead."

Your choice of words can tire your listener and date you. Friend and word maven Marion Glaser reminds us that we now say:

black tie instead of tuxedo
wall space instead of shelves
copier instead of carbon paper
server instead of waiter or waitress
console instead of switchboard
swimsuit instead of bathing suit
parking brake instead of emergency brake
hair stylist instead of beautician
letter carrier instead of postman
pharmacist instead of druggist
animal control officer instead of dogcatcher
funeral director instead of undertaker

Note: For more examples of out-of-it and with-it words check William Safire's book *I Stand Corrected*.

How's this for word awareness? A car dealer who grew tired of "pre-owned vehicles" for "used cars" decided to sell "nearly-new cars" and increased his sales dramatically.

# REDUNDANCIES

The superb communicator also achieves crisp language by avoiding verbiage.

Here are examples of redundancies:

a.m. in the morning
climb up
consensus of opinion (General consensus of opinion is even worse.)
continue on
doctorate degree
each and every
end result
equally as
few in number
final outcome
free gift
join together/mix together
Mount Katahdin (The word Katahdin means big mountain.)
new innovation (An innovation is a new method, idea or device.)
old adage/old proverb
past history
plan ahead
reason why
return back/revert back
Sahara Desert (The word Sahara means desert.)
Sierra Mountains (The word Sierra means mountain.)
Skirt around

F. Flag down the watch words.

The most dramatic way to become a superb communicator is to become acutely aware of the words you've stored in your word warehouse.

Those words are tools of the brain. You blunt them at your peril.

Please look carefully at the words flagged for your attention. For every wince word or phrase you eliminate, you will improve your speech by one percent. While this is by no means a complete list, there are more than 100 words for you to check. Master them and you will have achieved the 100 percent solution to word pollution.

**accept/except:** Accept is always a verb and has in it the idea of receiving or agreeing to. Except always conveys the idea of excluding or omitting.

**accidentally:** The word has five syllables. Accidently is an obsolete and no longer used spelling.

**affect/effect:** Affect means to influence. The result is an effect. Effect is also a verb meaning to bring about; cause. (By the way, there is a noun affect used in psychology, meaning a "feeling or emotion." It is pronounced with the accent on the first syllable.)

**aggravate:** To aggravate is to increase, make worse. Aggravate does not mean to irritate, although it is often so used colloquially.

**already/all ready:** Already is an adverb. Correct: Everyone had already arrived. The two words all ready mean that everyone or everything is prepared or all ready.

**alright:** A spelling much used but still generally considered substandard. Use all right.

**among:** Among should be used only when referring to more than two persons or things.

**angry at/angry with:** You are usually angry with a person and angry at happenings or things. It's always better to be angry with a person than mad at him or her.

**anxious:** Anxious means to be uneasy because of thoughts or fears about what could happen. Eager means wanting very much.

**anyplace:** Anyplace is incorrect for anywhere. It is all right to say, "She can go into any place on the street."

**anywhere:** Please do not say anywheres.

**at:** At should never be used with where. Wrong: I do not know where she's at. Right: I do not know where she is.

**athlete:** The word athlete has two syllables. Do not say ath-a-lete as some athletes do.

**author:** Author is a noun, and it refers to one who makes or originates something. Authors cringe when someone says, "He authored a book."

**ax:** Ax as the pronunciation of ask is wrong and has proved costly to job seekers and workers who seek promotion. Please say ask.

**between you and I:** Remember that between (as a preposition) takes an object and that object should be in the objective case. Wrong: between you and I. Right: between you and me.

**boughten:** Boughten means purchased. It is colloquial and to be avoided.

**Calvary/cavalry:** Calvary is the place near Jerusalem where Christ was crucified. Cavalry has to do with horses. I always remember the distinction between these two by associating Calvin, the Christian reformer, with the first and the word cavalier with the second.

**can't hardly:** Can't hardly is a double negative and should be avoided. Say can hardly.

**chasm:** The word is pronounced kaz-em.

**childish/childlike:** Childish means of, or similar to, or suitable for a child. When used to describe an adult, the word connotes foolishness. Childlike is a more positive word meaning like or befitting a child, innocent.

**complected:** A colloquial word. Complexioned is preferred.

**credible/credulous:** Credible means believable. Credulous means gullible, ready to believe. (Creditable has nothing to do with believing; it means deserving of credit or praise.)

**data:** Data is the plural of datum. It is correct to say these data are sufficient.

**December:** Please do not put a z sound in the word. It is not Dee-zember, but Dee-sember.

**elder/older:** We speak of a woman as older than her friend, the elder of two sisters and the eldest of her family. Elder and eldest are applied to persons only, while older and oldest are used of persons and things.

**enthused:** Enthused is still considered a colloquialism. Say I'm enthusiastic.

**escape:** Please do not put an x in this word. It is not pronounced excape. Say es-cape.

**espresso:** Please do not put an x in this word. It is es-press-so.

**et cetera:** Please do not put an x in this word. It is not ex cet-er-a. It is et cet-er-a. Don't you wonder how all these x's sneaked (not snuck) into our language?

**experiment:** There is no spear in this word. Say ek-sper-i-ment, not ek-SPEAR-i-ment.

**famed:** A substandard word for famous.

**farther/further:** Farther refers to measurable distance. Further, as an adjective, describes "a continuation, usually of time or degree." For example: She had further news. (As a verb further means to advance as in to further a career.)

**February:** The word is pronounced feb-roo-ary. Sound that first r. Yes, I know, Walter Cronkite persisted in dropping that first r. Countless listeners remarked on it. In fact, Ann Landers devoted a column to the word in order to answer all those who told her about the mispronunciation.

**fewer/less:** Say fewer when you refer to something that can be counted. Less means not so much. A book that has fewer words is less tiresome.

**fiscal/physical:** Fiscal, pronounced fis-kul, means of or pertaining to finance. Physical, pronounced fiz-uh-kul, pertains to the body.

**for free:** This is a phrase that annoys many listeners. Merely say "free" if it is.

**had of:** Had of is a vulgarism. Wrong: I wish I had of done it sooner. Right: I wish I had done it sooner.

**healthful/healthy:** Healthful means health giving. Healthy means possessing health.

**heartrending:** The word means causing much grief or anguish. The word has three syllables, not four. Do not say heartrendering. One renders fat, not hearts.

**here's two ways to:** It should be "Here **are** two ways to." If the sentence opening were recast without the contraction, it would read "Here is two ways to," and that would surely produce "hear-ache" in the listening ear.

**humble:** Sound the h in this word. It is humble, not umble.

**I don't think:** Say I think not instead.

**Illinois:** The word is pronounced il-uh-noi, never il-uh-noise.

**imply/infer:** Speakers and writers imply something by what they say; they do not infer. The listeners or readers infer something from the remarks of the speakers and writers. Do not say you are inferring when you mean you are implying.

**incidentally:** Note that the word has five syllables. It is not incidently. The word incidently has gone out of fashion.

**index:** Both the Latin and English plurals are used. Indices and indexes are both correct.

**individual:** The word individual should not be used indiscriminately for person. Strictly, an individual is a particular being as distinguished from a class or group.

**ingenious/ingenuous:** Ingenious means resourceful, clever, inventive. Ingenuous means frank, open, honest.

**in parenthesis:** No one can enclose an expression in one parenthesis; at least two parentheses are required.

**Italian:** Please do not say EYE-talian. There is no such word. Think of the word Italy and it won't trouble you; you wouldn't say Eyetaly. I include this word for Joseph Tinervia of McGraw-Hill.

**it's/its:** It's stands for it is, or it has. Its means belonging to it. It's and its have made every list of language errors I've seen. It's imperative that you get it right.

**invite:** Invite is a verb. One doesn't issue an invite. One issues an invitation.

**jewelry:** The root of this word is jewel. Be sure to include jewel in your pronunciation of the word. Say jewel-ree.

**lay/lie:** Lay and lie are two different verbs. Confusion arises because the past tense of the verb lie is lay. Lay is a transitive verb; it means to place. You lay a book on a desk or a hen lays an egg. The past tense and past participle of lay are laid. Lie is an intransitive verb; it means to take a reclining position. The past participle is lain. Lie is also another intransitive verb, meaning to tell a falsehood. The past tense and past participle of this verb are lied. There is also a nautical verb lay, but this is confusing enough without that one.

**learn/teach:** Never use learn to mean instruct. Wrong: I'll learn you to behave. Right: I'll teach you to behave.

**leave/let:** It is idiomatic to say, "Leave him alone." Right: "Let him alone."

**library:** Please pronounce the r in the middle. It is lie-brair-ee.

**like:** Please do not use the word like as a filler. It's a conversational burr that seems to have a permanent place in the speech patterns of people who can't utter two sentences without saying like.

**manufacture:** The second syllable of the word is u. It is not uh. Say man-you-fac-chur.

**meantime/meanwhile:** Remember "meanwhile, back at the ranch," and you won't confuse these two. Meanwhile is an adverb, a word used to describe an action; meantime is a noun. Therefore, you can't say in the meanwhile, or meantime, back at the ranch.

**mischievous:** This word has three syllables. There is no such word as miss-chee-vee-ous. Learn to spell the word and you'll say it correctly. It's mis-chi-vus.

**most:** Most should not be used in place of almost.

**noisome:** Noisome means offensive, particularly with reference to odors. Do not use it to mean somewhat noisy.

**nuclear:** The word is pronounced noo-klee-ur, not noo-cue-ler. I'm told that three of our presidents mispronounced this word. Of course no one outranked them so they continued to mispronounce nuclear.

**once:** There is no such word as onct. Please say once.

**oral:** Oral means spoken. It is not interchangeable with verbal. Verbal can mean spoken or it can refer to something that is written.

**out loud:** Aloud is preferable.

**partial:** Because this word can indicate preference, its use to indicate incompleteness can be ambiguous and should be avoided. Use part or partly, depending on the context.

**persecute/prosecute:** Both words describe negative actions, but persecute means to oppress, molest, bother. Prosecute means to sue, indict, arraign, pursue.

**principal/principle:** Principal as an adjective, means the most important. Principal may also be used as a noun, referring to a leader or chief, as to the principal of a school. Principle is never an adjective; as a noun, the word means a fundamental truth, a rule, a law. One would say the principle of honesty is best.

**prone:** Describes lying flat with the face down. It should not be used instead of supine. Supine means lying back with the face upward.

**prophecy/prophesy:** Prophecy is the noun. Prophesy is the verb. One could say the prophecy was false. He prophesied that they would marry but he was wrong, they didn't even like each other.

**prostate/prostrate:** Prostate is a gland. Prostrate means stretched out, prone or supine.

**raise/rear:** Raise, meaning to grow or breed, is commonly used when speaking of nonhuman objects, as plants or animals. One rears children.

**Realtor:** Realtor is pronounced real-tor, not ree-la-tor. Note that the a comes before the l. Realtor refers to an agent affiliated with the National Association of Real Estate boards. The word Realtor is capitalized.

**recognize:** The word has a g in the middle. Let's hear it. Do not say rek-on-ize. It is rek-ug-nize.

**recur:** It is correct to say recur rather than reoccur.

**regime/regimen:** Regime means rule. Regimen means routine. So you don't follow a regime of diet and exercise; it is a regimen.

**sacrilegious.** The word is often misspelled. Do not associate it with religion. The word is related to sacrilege. Pronounce it sak-ree-lee-jus.

**sanatorium/sanitarium:** Although the terms are interchangeable, in ordinary use, the first is thought of as a health-restoring place of whatever kind, but the second connotes a place where prophylactic treatment is predominant.

**sherbet:** Please don't insert a second r in the word. It is sher-bet, not sher-bert.

**suspicion:** You have a suspicion; you suspect. Do not say, "I suspicion."

**swam/swum:** Swam is the preferred past tense of swim. He swam across the pool. Swum is the preferred participial form. He has swum across the pool before.

**temperature:** Be sure to pronounce all four syllables. And do not say, "Billy had a temperature," when you mean that Billy had a fever. Of course Billy had a temperature. Every living being has a temperature.

**theater:** The word is pronounced thee-uh-ter, not thee-aye-ter.

**theirselves:** Theirselves is an erroneous substitute for themselves.

**those kind:** Those denotes a plural word. Say those kinds.

**unbeknownst:** Unbeknownst is an awkward dialectical substitute for unknown or without knowledge.

**undoubtedly:** Do not say this word as though it were undoubtably. It is un-dou-ted-ly. Let's hear the ted.

**unique:** The word unique means one of a kind, therefore it does not take a modifier. It is not **so** unique or **quite** unique.

**Washington:** The first syllable has no r in it. It is not worsh-ing-ton. Nor does the word wash have an r in it.

**ways:** Ways is incorrect when preceded by an article or adjective which is singular. Wrong: Go down this road a little ways. Right: Go down this road a little way.

G. Use the correct abbreviations for state names.

Because we are accustomed to e-mail, it's easy to forget some of the rules governing the sending of snail mail—especially the states whose names have similar beginnings. States such as Minnesota, Mississippi, Michigan, and Minnesota are particularly nettlesome in this regard.

Before addressing thank you notes, invitations, or greeting cards, take a look at this communicator's aid. With these guidelines, you'll not only have better postal service, you'll seem more savvy to recipients of other written material. Keep this chart handy. I do.

## ABBREVIATING STATE NAMES

Abbreviations for the names of states evolved as a convenience, without standardization. Traditionally, the names of a few states are not abbreviated. (These exceptions are noted by an * in the table below.)

These abbreviations should not be used in text when standing alone, but are usually used in lists or tables.

The U.S. Postal Service introduced a set of standard abbreviations, consisting of two capital letters without periods, for use in addressing mail. These abbreviations are unambiguous and are suitable for optical character recognition and machine-sorting of mail. The postal service abbreviations should always be used in addresses. Many editors and style manuals object to use of postal service abbreviations in any other context, but they are fighting a losing battle.

| Name of state | Postal service abbreviation | Common abbreviation |
|---|---|---|
| Alaska | AK | * |
| Alabama | AL | Ala. |
| Arizona | AZ | Ariz. |
| Arkansas | AR | Ark. |
| California | CA | Cal. or Calif. |
| Colorado | CO | Colo. |
| Connecticut | CT | Conn. |
| Delaware | DE | Del. |
| Florida | FL | Fla. |
| Georgia | GA | Ga. |
| Hawaii | HI | * |
| Idaho | ID | * |
| Illinois | IL | Ill. |
| Indiana | IN | Ind. |
| Iowa | IA | * |
| Kansas | KS | Kans. |

| | | |
|---|---|---|
| Kentucky | KY | Ky. |
| Louisiana | LA | La. |
| Maine | ME | * |
| Maryland | MD | Md. |
| Massachusetts | MA | Mass. |
| Michigan | MI | Mich. |
| Minnesota | MN | Minn. |
| Mississippi | MS | Miss. |
| Missouri | MO | Mo. |
| Montana | MT | Mont. |
| North Carolina | NC | N.C. |
| North Dakota | ND | N.Dak. |
| Nebraska | NE | Neb. or Nebr. |
| Nevada | NV | Nev. |
| New Hampshire | NH | N.H. |
| New Jersey | NJ | N.J. |
| New Mexico | NM | N.Mex. |
| New York | NY | N.Y. |
| Ohio | OH | * |
| Oklahoma | OK | Okla. |
| Oregon | OR | Ore. or Oreg. |
| Pennsylvania | PA | Pa. or Penn. |
| Rhode Island | RI | R.I. |
| South Carolina | SC | S.C. |
| South Dakota | SD | S.Dak. |
| Tennessee | TN | Tenn. |
| Texas | TX | Tex. |
| Utah | UT | * |
| Virginia | VA | Va. |
| Vermont | VT | Vt. |
| Washington | WA | Wash. |
| West Virginia | WV | W.Va. |
| Wisconsin | WI | Wis. or Wisc. |
| Wyoming | WY | Wyo. |

Abbreviations of states following the names of cities are enclosed in commas when the common forms are used, but commas may be omitted with the postal service abbreviations.

# PART IV

As the World Terms
    Quips, Quotes and Savvy Sayings about the Way the World Wags

# AS THE WORLD TERMS

As you will see from comments made by the famous and not so famous our world wags in much the same manner it did when Shakespeare first commented on "how the world wags" in *As You Like It*.

## Advice

Your temper is one of your most valuable possessions. Don't lose it.

After his team lost, a Southern football coach was told, "The last train leaves town at dusk. Be under it."

Say the best and think the rest.

Talent is God given, be grateful. Reputation is man given, be humble. Ego is self given, be careful.

If the shoe fits, buy it.

E. Hubbard gave this advice: "The greatest mistake you can make in life is to be continually fearing you will make one."

Consider the source. Deciding whether it is from one who is admirable or one who is envious will help you in your response.

If you can't say something nice, say it nicely.

John Charlton Collins offered this: "To profit from good advice requires more wisdom than to give it."

Sing and talk in the key of B natural.

From listening comes wisdom. From speaking comes repentance.

Smart cookies don't crumble.

You can't win a prize in a contest you haven't entered.

Whatever your lot in life, build something on it.

If you want your dreams to come true, don't sleep so much.

Your best personality is the one that's already inside you. Free yourself enough to be yourself.

Listen to your heart talk. Be heartheaded.

When you stretch the truth, it snaps back.
When you wave at me use all your fingers.
To save face keep the lower half shut.

From masseuse Maureen Tozier we have this advice: "It's best to use different strokes for different folks." She also said, "Keep in touch."

Finley Peter Dunne advises, "Trust everybody—but cut the cards."

## America

America is hero hungry and wimp weary.

## Anger

According to Horace, "a brief lunacy."
According to Hosea Ballou, "Mental imbecility."

## British

The British say that "one for the road" refers to the criminal's last drink before he is marched to his execution.

## Bumper Sticker

Phyllis Eveleigh is still chuckling over this one she spotted ages ago: Down With Hot Pants.

## Courage

Courage is not the absence of fear; it is the mastery of it.

## Credit

Real people do not take credit, they give it.

## Criticism

Proverbs 9:8—Do not reprove a scoffer or he will hate you. Reprove a wise man and he will love you.

Criticism is something we can avoid easily—by saying nothing, doing nothing, and being nothing.—Aristotle

## Death

"It is not death, it is dying that alarms me."—Michel E. Montaigne

"The good die first; and they whose hearts are as dry as summer dust burn to the socket."—Wordsworth

"He whom the gods love, dies young."—Menander (Athenian dramatist whose first name seems to have eluded historians—and me)

Similarly E. Hubbard said, "Whom the gods love die young no matter how long they live."

Longfellow had this to say on the subject of death, "There is no death! What seems so is transition; this life of mortal breath is but a suburb of the life elysian, whose portal we call death."

Walter Scott said, "Is death the last sleep? No, it is the last and final awakening."

"Each departed friend is like a magnet that attracts us to the next world."—Jean Paul Richter

"This world is the land of the dying; the next is the land of the living."—Tryon Edwards

Milton maintained that "Death is the golden key that opens the palace of eternity."

## Education

Sir Josiah Stamp said that education is "the inculcation of the incomprehensible into the ignorant by the incompetent."

Oscar Wilde said that education is "an admirable thing but it is well to remember that nothing worth knowing can be taught."

## Envy

"Envy, the meanest of vices, creeps on the ground like a serpent."—Ovid

## Epitaph

Epitaph for a waiter: God finally caught his eye.

Life's a jest, and all things show it, I thought so once, and now I know it.—John Gay

## Famous people

Famous people made remarkable remarks.

From Fred Allen we have: "Hanging is too good for a man who makes puns. He should be drawn and quoted."

Maya Angelou said, "Start loving yourself before you ask someone else to love you."

Sam Goldwyn said, "Include me out."

"I cook with wine. Sometimes I even add it to the food."—W. C. Fields

John Hancock said, "A chip on the shoulder is too heavy a piece of baggage to carry through life."

Oliver Wendell Holmes said, "Most men go to their graves with the music still inside."

Will Mayo declined a chance for partnership with a Park Avenue doctor. He said he'd settle for a country practice with his father in Rochester, Minnesota.

Dolly Parton said she didn't mind those dumb blonde jokes because she wasn't dumb and she wasn't blonde.

Will Rogers told us to "Love people and use things, not the other way around." He also told us that he'd never met a man he didn't like. Mae West reportedly said that she hadn't either.

Mae West also said, "Between two evils, I choose the one I haven't tried." And she said, "When I'm good, I'm very, very good but when I'm bad, I'm better."

In a United Features Syndicate piece we are told that Charles M. Schultz said, "A good education is the next best thing to a pushy mother." He also said, "Life is easier if you dread it only one day at a time." And that "Life is like an ice-cream cone: you have to learn to lick it."

## Fashion

We should forgive fashion anything. It dies so quickly.

Thoreau said, "Every generation laughs at the old fashion, but follows religiously the new."

**Fear**

"There is a time to take counsel of your fears, and there is a time to never listen to any fear."—General George S. Patton

**Fictional characters**

Fictional characters made interesting remarks.

In *Gone With the Wind*, Rhett Butler told Scarlett, "You should be kissed, and often, and by someone who knows how."

Sherlock Holmes made this remark: "I cannot agree with those who rank modesty among the virtues."

**Folly**

"There is a foolish corner even in the brain of the sage."—Aristotle

"He who lives without folly is not so wise as he imagines."—Rochefoucauld

Too much trust is folly in an imperfect world.

Every day an average of four people call Graceland and ask to speak to Elvis.

**Forgiveness**

"Forgiveness is man's deepest need and highest achievement."—Horace Bushnell

**God**

Godly remarks include the following:

Ben Hooper, Governor of Tennessee, told us, "In God's plan, every person is a first-round draft choice. If you don't think you're worth much, you're going to have an argument with God."

Never mind that you don't believe in God. He still believes in you.

Francis Cardinal Spellman advised us to "Pray as if everything depends on God, and work as if everything depended on you."

When you get to your wit's end, you'll find God lives there.

God doesn't call the qualified, He qualifies the called.

"God is not a cosmic bellboy for whom we can press a button to get things."—Harry Emerson Fosdick

Prayer at both ends of the day keeps the day from unraveling in the middle.

Wilson Mizner said, "I respect faith, but doubt is what gets you an education."

When your knees shake, kneel on them.

Maya Angelou tells us, "We all come from the Creator, each human being streaming with glory."

A website offering: "What should a good sermon be about? About God and about ten minutes."

## Graduate

To the graduate—"Remember: It's a diploma, not a passport."

According to Robert M. Hutchins, a graduate is one who completes a college course and "is presented with a sheepskin to cover his intellectual nakedness."

## Hope

"Hope is a pathological belief in the occurrence of the impossible."—H. L. Menken

## Humor

"Humor is the sunshine of the mind."—Edward Bulwer-Lytton

## Life

According to Mark Twain, "The first half of life consists of the capacity to enjoy without the chance; the last half consists of the chance without the capacity."

According to Fred Ebb who wrote the lyrics for *Cabaret*, "Life is a cabaret, old chum. Life is a cabaret."

Voltaire told us, "We never live; we are always in the expectation of living."

Goethe told us, "Life is the childhood of our immortality." Goethe also maintained that "A useless life is only an early death."

James A. Barrie told us that "Life is a long lesson in humility."

Oscar Wilde had this to say about life: "The Book of Life begins with a man and a woman in a garden. It ends with Revelations."

The following is attributed to Samuel Johnson: "A book should teach us to enjoy life, or endure it."

Hans Christian Andersen said, "Every man's life is a fairy tale written by God's fingers."

Oliver Wendell Holmes said this about life: "With most men life is like backgammon—half skill and half luck."

Carlos Wilcox made this profound remark: "It is an infamy to die and not be missed."

Theodore Roosevelt warned that "The poorest way to face life is to face it with a sneer."

Samuel Butler said, "Life is the art of drawing sufficient conclusions from insufficient premises."

## Marriage

The best romance is inside marriage. The finest love stories come after the wedding.

"Love is blind, but marriage is a real eye-opener." Quoted by Paula Deen on the Food Network.

## Men

Men are afraid of failure. Women are afraid of success.

One's a leg man, the other is a chest nut.

The man who thinks he's smart has a smart wife.

Seneca said, "Men are but children, too, though they have grey hairs; they are only of a larger size."

## Observations

Mind set is more like mind lock.

There's no justice in the world. Thank goodness.

Most worries are reruns.

You can't turn back the clock. But you can wind it up again.

The sole purpose of a child's middle name is so he can tell when he's really in trouble.

"A parent never wakes up the second baby just to see it smile."—Grace Williams

Angels can fly because they take themselves lightly.

When you choose the beginning of a road, you choose the end of it as well.

Memory is the power to gather roses in winter.

A cat that once sat on a hot stove won't sit on a cold one either.

Everyone has a right to my opinion.

A fanatic doubles his efforts after he has lost sight of the goal.

The longest hour has only sixty minutes.

Happiness is an inside job.

Nostalgia is big business—a yearning for a time that never was.

A diplomat has been defined as a person who makes you feel at home even when he wishes you were.

Some people have to have someone else's name on their clothes or they think they're nobody.

From Ambrose Bierce we learn, "Calamities are of two kinds; misfortune to ourselves, and good fortune to others."

A penny saved is a government oversight.

Uneasy lies the head that wears the crown.

It's nice to be kneaded.

We don't need to see eye to eye but heart to heart.

David Belasco said, "If you can't write your idea on the back of my calling card, you don't have a clear idea."

When all's said and done, there's more said than done.

"The world is a comedy to those who think, a tragedy to those who feel," according to Horace Walpole.

## Old Age

One of the questions addressed to President Reagan during his campaign was concerned with age and Mr. Reagan's ability to do the job. He replied, "I am not going to make age an issue in this campaign. I am not going to exploit for political purposes my opponent's youth and inexperience."

Barnard M. Baruch said that old age is "always fifteen years older than I am."

When Frank Lloyd Wright (at age 83) was asked to name his greatest achievement, he said, "My next one."

It's better to be "over the hill" than under it.

Joyce and Bill Shewman remind us that "Retirement is not for sissies."

Thanks to the Reverend Larry H. Pigg for sending these inspired words of Longfellow's:

> "It is too late!" Ah, nothing is too late—
> Cato learned Greek at eighty; Sophocles
> Wrote his grand "Oedipus," and Simonides
> Bore off the prize of verse from his compeers
> When each had numbered more than fourscore years;
> And Theophrastus, at fourscore and ten,
> Had begun his "Characters of Men."
> Chaucer, at Woodstock, with his nightingales,
> At sixty wrote the "Canterbury Tales."
> Goethe, at Weimar, toiling to the last,
> Completed "Faust" when eighty years were past.
> What then? Shall we sit idly down and say,
> "The night has come; it is no longer day?"
> For age is opportunity no less
> Than youth itself, though in another dress.
> And as the evening twilight fades away,
> The sky is filled with stars, invisible by day.
> It is never too late to start doing what is right.
> Never.

## Power

Being powerful is like being a lady. If you have to tell people you are, you aren't.

Avoid the victim's stance. Don't offer yourself for approval.

At times silence is power. Wait 'em out.

## Realist

The pessimist complains about the wind. The optimist expects it to change. The realist adjusts the sails.

## Relationships

He who pulls on the oars doesn't have time to rock the boat.

It's difficult to teach an old relationship new tricks.

Love is the only sane and satisfactory answer to the problem of human existence.

## Vanity

Vanity is a vice that hurts no one. Envy hurts everyone.

But vanity is sanity.

## Woman

She managed to be shrewd without being shrewish.

She who laughs lasts.

"A woman's lot is made for her by the love she accepts."—George Eliot

"Men have sight; women insight."—Victor Hugo

A woman wants to be weighed and found wanting.

Women who want to be equal to men have no ambition.

## Writer

"The writer does the most who gives his reader the most knowledge, and takes from him the least time."—Sydney Smith

# PART V

Terms to Tempt the Creative Communicator
    Eponyms, words derived from the names of people
    Animal Talk
    Small Talk

# EPONYMS—NAMES THAT BECAME WORDS

Let's look deeply at the words derived from the names of people. There is often a message behind the person as well as a person behind the message.

After looking at the list of eponyms, look at the way creative speakers have been inspired by eponyms. Do study your own name to see if it can be used creatively. Then, look inside yourself to see what can be brought forth to make your name memorable.

I thought I had garnered an impressive list of eponyms until a friend asked if I'd included the word "Clintonesque." He explained that clintonesque refers to not being straightforward. He cited Clinton's evasive hedging about "what the meaning of is is" as an example.

Stay with me for as complete a list of eponyms as you're likely to find. I do realize that as I write more eponyms are being born. I am also aware that there are around 35,000 of the things out there. In medicine a name of a drug, structure, or disease based on or derived from the name of a person is an eponym. Your best bet is to consult a medical dictionary for such terms.

**ampere** (After A. M. Ampère, French physicist) Ampere is the standard unit for measuring the strength of an electric current.

**begonia** (After Michel Begon, French botanist) Begonia refers to a plant with white, pink, or red flowers, having ornamental leaves.

**bloomer** (After Amelia Bloomer, American feminist) A bloomer formerly referred to a woman's garment consisting of a skirt and loose trousers gathered at the ankles. Now it usually refers to a garment with baggy trousers gathered at the knees. I must say it's rare to see bloomers on today's female athletes. And, Amelia wouldn't recognize the undergarments we call bloomers.

**blurb** A blurb refers to the book industry's term for frequently puffed-up expressions of high praise that grace the jackets of books. The word blurb was coined by the American humorist Gelett Burgess, and it was named for Belinda Blurb, a model for a special book jacket. Burgess wrote more than 35 books, but I'll bet most of you will remember him for his whimsical verse. Burgess is responsible for:

> I never saw a purple cow
>
> I never hope to see one.
>
> But I can tell you anyhow
>
> I'd rather see than be one.

I can't resist adding that Burgess became so weary of hearing that little verse, he later added this rejoinder:

> Ah yes, I wrote the "Purple Cow"—
>
> I'm sorry now I wrote it!
>
> But I can tell you anyhow,
>
> I'll kill you if you quote it.

**bobby** (After Sir Robert Peel) Sir Robert Peel remodeled the London police force. Bobby has become British slang for policeman.

**boycott** (After Charles C. Boycott, Irish land agent) Boycott was ostracized by tenants for refusing to lower his outrageous rents. Today boycott means to refuse to buy or use something.

**camellia** (Named for Georg Josef Kamel, Moravian Jesuit missionary) 1. An evergreen tree or shrub of the tea family. 2. The flower of a camellia, also called japonica.

**cardigan** (Named after the 7th Earl of Cardigan) A cardigan is usually a knitted woolen sweater that opens down the front. You history buffs will also remember the 7th Earl of Cardigan as the British general who led the Light Brigade of British cavalry against the Russians in the Battle of Balaklava, October 25, 1854, during the Crimean War—an incident immortalized in Alfred Lord Tennyson's poem "The Charge of the Light Brigade" (1855). By spending an estimated 10,000 pounds a year from his private purse, Cardigan made his regiment the smartest in the service. Yes, that's when he introduced what came to be called the cardigan jacket.

**chauvinism** (After Nicolas Chauvin, Napoleonic soldier known for his fanatical patriotism) 1. Fanatical patiotism. 2. Unreasoning devotion to one's sex or race, etc.

**chesterfield** (After the Earl of Chesterfield) A chesterfield is a single-breasted topcoat, usually with concealed buttons and a velvet collar.

**clerihew** (Invented by E. Clerihew Bentley, English writer) Clerihew refers to a humorous quatrain about a person—the person is usually named in the first line.

**clintonesque** See comments in the third paragraph of the introduction to these eponyms.

**Cobb salad** A salad named for Bob Cobb, owner of the Brown Derby restaurant in Los Angeles. Mr. Cobb introduced his salad in 1926.

**daguerreotype** (Invented by Louis J. M. Daguerre) Daguerreotype refers to a photograph made by an early method on a chemically treated metal or glass.

**dahlia** (Named for Anders Dahl, Swedish botanist) Dahlia is a perennial plant of the composite family, with tuberous roots and large showy flowers.

**davenport** (Named for the original manufacturer) A davenport refers to a large sofa. It is sometimes convertible into a bed. The British refer to a small desk as a davenport.

**derrick** (Named for Thomas Derrick, who worked as an executioner at London's Tyburn gallows) Derrick refers to a large crane for hoisting and moving heavy objects. It can also refer to a tall framework over the opening of a drilled hole. Derrick was convicted of rape and condemned to die. The Earl of Essex, who pardoned him, was executed in 1601 for treason. He was executed by Derrick. How's that for irony?

**derringer** (Invented by Henry Derringer, American gunsmith) Derringer refers to a short-barreled pistol with a large bore.

**diesel engine** (Invented by Rudolph Diesel) A diesel engine refers to a type of internal combustion engine that burns oil.

**doily** (Named for Doyly or Doily, a London draper) A doily refers to a small mat made of lace, linen or paper. It is used to protect or adorn furniture.

**draconian** (Named for Draco) Draco was an Athenian lawgiver whose harsh code punished both trivial and serious crimes with death. Hence, the continued use of the word draconian to describe oppressive measures.

**dunce** (A contemptuous reference to the followers of John Duns Scotus) A dunce is said to be a stupid person, a person who learns more slowly than others. Praise be that teachers no longer put "dunce caps" on their slow-learning or obstreperous students.

**Fahrenheit** (After Gabriel Fahrenheit, German physicist) Fahrenheit refers to a temperature scale in which the boiling point of pure water is 212° and the freezing point is 32°.

**forsythia** (After William Forsyth, English botanist) Forsythia refers to any of several shrubs of the genus Forsythia, native to Asia, and cultivated for their early-blooming, yellow bell-shaped flowers.

**fuchsia** (After Leonard Fuchs, German botanist) Fuchsia is a shrub of the evening primrose family, with pink, red or purple flowers. Fuchsia also refers to a purplish-red color.

**galvanic** (After Luigi Galvani) Pertaining to direct-current electricity, it also means having the effect of an electric shock.

**gardenia** (Named for Dr. Alexander Garden) A gardenia is a white or yellowish flower with fragrant, waxy petals or the shrub bearing this flower.

**Gatling gun** (Designed by Richard J. Gatling, American inventor) A Gatling gun is a machine gun having a cluster of barrels fired as the cluster is turned. Gat (a shortening of Gatling) is slang for a pistol.

**gaudy** Modernists say that the word gaudy is influenced by Antonio Gaudi, the famous Catalan architect. Gaudi's distinctive style is characterized by voluptuous color and texture. Those who study language say the word gaudy has an earlier history and comes from the French gaudir. Still others say it comes from the Latin guadere. I find myself using the word gaudy instead of the fancier word ostentatious.

**Geiger counter** (After Hans Geiger, German physicist) A Geiger counter is an instrument used for detecting and counting ionizing particles as from radioactive ores.

**gentian** (Probably after Gentius, king of Illyria—second century B.C.) Gentian refers to any of numerous plants of the genus Gentiana, the bitter root of the yellow gentian.

**gerrymander** (Derived from the name Gerry, last name of Eldridge Gerry) The word comes from Gerry plus (sala)mander from the shape of an election district created while Gerry was governor of Massachusetts 1810-1811. Gerrymander now means to divide a voting district in such a way as to give unfair advantage to one political party.

**grangerize** (After J. Granger, English biographer, who wrote *Biographical History of England* 1769) To grangerize is to illustrate a book with drawings or prints taken from other books. Granger's *Biographical History of England* was illustrated in this manner.

**guillotine** (After Joseph Ignace Guillotin, French doctor who suggested its use) A guillotine is a machine with a heavy blade that falls freely between upright guides in order to behead a condemned prisoner.

**hansom** (After J.A. Hansom, English inventor) The hansom is a two-wheeled covered carriage for two passengers. It is pulled by one horse.

**havelock** (After Sir Henry Havelock, British general who served in India) A havelock is a cloth covering for a cap. It has a flap to protect the back of the neck.

**Linnaean** (After Carolus Linnaeus, Swedish botanist) You might not use the name of this system for classifying plants and animals, but you use the common names derived from the scientific names. Look at all the flowers on this list.

**leotard** (Popularized by Jules Leotard, 10th century French aerialist) A leotard is a snug, elastic garment originally worn by dancers and acrobats.

**Levis** (After Levi Strauss, the American manufacturer) Levis is a trademark for snugly fitting trousers of heavy denim with rivets reinforcing points of strain.

**loganberry** (Named for James H. Logan, American horticulturist) The Loganberry is a hybrid bramble developed from the blackberry and the red raspberry.

**lynch** (After James Lynch, 18th century Virginia planter and justice of the peace) To lynch is to execute without due process of law; especially to hang.

**macadam** (Developed by John L. McAdam, Scottish engineer) It refers to compacted small stones used in making roads.

**mackintosh** (Named for its inventor, Charles Macintosh, Scottish chemist) A mackintosh is a waterproof outer coat.

**magnolia** (After Pierre Magnol, French botanist) Magnolia refers to any of a group of trees or shrubs with large, fragrant flowers of white, pink or purple. It also refers to the flower.

**martinet** (After Jean Martinet, 17th century French general) A martinet is a very strict disciplinarian.

**masochism** (After Leopold von Sacher-Masoch, Austrian novelist who described it) It means deriving of abnormal sexual pleasure from being dominated or pained.

**maudlin** (From Mary Magdaline—various spellings of Magdalene or Maudeleyne) To be maudlin is to be tearfully sentimental.

**mausoleum** (Originally referred to the tomb of Mausolus, king of an ancient land in Asia Minor) Mausoleum refers to a large imposing tomb or a building housing such a tomb or tombs.

**maverick** (After Samuel Maverick, 19th century Texas cattleman who did not brand his cattle) The term refers to an unbranded animal or to a person who acts in an independent manner.

**Mercerize** (Named for John Mercer, English calico dealer) Mercerize means to treat cotton thread or fabric with sodium hydroxide, so as to shrink the fiber and increase its color absorption.

**mesmerize** (After Franz Anton Mesmer, Austrian physician) To mesmerize is to hypnotize or to suggest a hypnotic state.

**napoleon** (After Napoleon I) A napoleon is a French pastry with a cream filling. It can also refer to a former gold coin of France or to a card game. I'll take the cream-filled pastry.

**nicotine** (Named for J. Nicot, 16th century French diplomat who introduced tobacco into France) Nicotine is a poisonous alkaloid derived from the tobacco plant, used in medicine and as an insecticide.

**ohm** (After G.S. Ohm, German Physicist) An ohm is a unit of electrical resistance.

**pasteurize** (After Louis Pasteur, French chemist and bacteriologist) To pasteurize is to destroy or check bacteria on milk, beer etc. by heating the liquid to 142-145° Fahrenheit for thirty minutes.

**pinchbeck** (Named for Christopher Pinchbeck) 1. An alloy of zinc and copper used as imitation gold. 2. An imitation.

**poinsettia** (Discovered by J.R. Poinsett, a U.S. minister to Mexico) The poinsettia is a Mexican and South American shrub with small flowers surrounded by petal-like red leaves.

**pompadour** (After Marquise de Pompadour, who was mistress of Louis XV of France) The pompadour is a hairdo in which the hair is swept up high from the forehead.

**praline** (Named for Marshal Duplessis-Pralin, whose cook invented it) It is a candy made of nuts, browned in boiling syrup.

**Pullman** (Named after G.M. Pullman, American inventor) Pullman refers to a Pullman car—either a parlor car or a sleeping car. Also, pullman is an adjective for a long narrow architectural feature such as a hall or kitchen.

**Quisling** (After Vidkun Quisling, a Norwegian who collaborated with the Nazis) A quisling is a person who betrays his own country by helping the enemy.

**raglan** (After Lord Raglan, British soldier) Raglan refers to a loose coat or sweater with slanted shoulder seams and with the sleeves extending in one piece to the neckline.

**ritzy** You're probably not surprised to learn that the word ritzy comes from the Ritz hotels. Swiss-born Cesar Ritz founded the hotels. His elegant Ritz hotels soon became a byword for luxurious living, and to "put on the ritz" meant to attempt to outshine others with a dazzling display of wealth or social position.

**sadistic** (After Comte Donatien de Sade, French writer who expounded principles of sexual violence) It means deliberately cruel—especially if associated with sex.

**sandwich** (Named after the 4th Earl of Sandwich) A sandwich consists of two or more slices of bread with meat, cheese or filling placed between them. Originally, sandwiches were made for the Earl of Sandwich so he could stay at the gambling table and not have to leave it for a meal.

**saxophone** (Invented by Adolphe Sax) A saxophone is a wind instrument having a single-reed mouthpiece, a curved metal body and a deep, mellow tone.

**sequoia** (Named after the Indian leader Sequoia) It refers to any very large evergreen tree of the genus Sequoia, which includes the redwood and the giant sequoias.

**shrapnel** (Named after the inventor General Henry Shrapnel, British artillery officer) The original shrapnel contained many small metal balls that were scattered when the shell exploded. The term now refers to the scattered fragments of the shell itself.

**sideburns** (Named for Ambrose Burnside) 1. Short whiskers grown only on the cheeks. 2. The hair growing on the face near the ears.

**silhouette** (After Etienne de Silhouette, 18th century French statesman) A silhouette is a representation of the outline of something—often a profile. It is usually filled in with black or another solid color.

**spoonerism** (After the Rev. W.A. Spooner) The Reverend William Spooner was an ordained Anglican priest and for fifty years an Oxford college don. All of this is forgotten because of his penchant for transposing sounds. Here are examples: "Son, it's kisstomary to cuss the bride," when he meant to say, "Son, it's customary to kiss the bride." He referred to "Our shoving leopard" when he meant to say, "Our loving shepherd." And one of the most widely quoted is, "Our queer old dean," when he meant to say, "Our dear old queen."

Even though the following are not true spoonerisms, The Reverend Spooner is remembered for saying to a troublesome undergraduate, "You will leave by the next drain." He also amused an entire audience by explaining to them that in his sermon when he said "Aristotle" he referred to St. Paul. Doubtless he meant to say apostle, not Aristotle.

While not so famous as Mr. Spooner, there exists a radio announcer who is remembered for saying, "Always demand the breast in bed." Poor man was doing a bread commercial and meant to say, "Always demand the best in bread."

**tawdry** (From tawdry lace, referring to laces sold at St. Audrey's fair, Norwich, England) Tawdry means gaudy, cheap, showy, sleazy.

**teddy bear** (Named after Theodore [Teddy] Roosevelt) A teddy bear is a child's toy somewhat like a small stuffed bear.

**victoria** (After Queen Victoria) It is a low, four-wheeled carriage for two passengers.

**volt** (After Count Alexander Volta 1745-1827, Italian physicist) A volt is the unit of electromotive force.

**watt** (After James Watt 1736-1819, Scottish inventor) A watt is a unit of electric power.

**wisteria** (After Caspar Wister or Wistar, American anatomist) Wisteria is a twining shrub of the pea family, with clusters of drooping purplish or white flowers.

**zeppelin** (After its inventor Count Ferdinand von Zeppelin) A zeppelin is a type of rigid dirigible.

**zinnia** (Named for J.G. Zinn, 18th century German botanist and physician) Zinnia refers to any of several plants of the aster family having colorful composite flowers.

Special note to you who make presentations: Your audience will long remember you if you're creative enough to turn your name into an eponym.

Examples:
Professor Young was in a playful mood one day and referred to his students as "Youngsters." The phrase caught on and was a factor in his increased popularity.

Professor Long captured his audience by using "Longings" as memory guides. Result: Long lines before a talk and Long lines afterward.

The Reverend Willie Strayhorn asked me to help his teenagers with their job campaigns. He referred to them as "Phyllis-teens." I latched onto his clever introduction and made reference to the Biblical Philistines. Then I urged them to become my kind of "Phyllis-teens."

I turned my last name, Martin, into Martechnique and used it as a heading, "The Martechnique of Time Management," in my book *Martin's Magic Motivation Book*.

You get the idea. A Smith could talk about Smithereens. One named Harmon could suggest that having her around would produce "harmony." A man named Benjamin reports success when offering **ben-a-fits**. And a young woman named Suhr came up with **suhr-prizes** for her clients. Her name provided an unexpected boon to her business. Even if your name is long or unusual, you can extract a syllable or two and coin a word or phrase from it.

Now that we've come this far, let's not "name drop." How's this for technique? My job seekers with names such as Hope, Love, Faith and Worth have told prospective employers to hire them else they, the employers, would be Hopeless, Loveless, Faithless or Worthless without them. The success rate on this has been gratifyingly awesome.

David Hammer of the Associated Press tells us that people are coming from the Presidential Library in Little Rock, Arkansas saying they're making a "Billgramage" to Arkansas.

I've merely skimmed the surface of possibilities here; you can do better.

# ANIMAL TALK

Let's talk of animals.
They have such taking ways.
A purr, a bark, adds just the spark
To brighten all our days.

This portion of the book is dedicated to our cat Penny. Penny is "penny wise" but she's far from "pound foolish." I say that because Penny wouldn't let us leave the pound without her. This despite our intention to shop around before deciding on **the** cat we wanted to adopt. In fact, we'd planned a visit to the Scratching Post the next day. We were told we couldn't be sure the pound would still have Penny if we didn't take her immediately. That and Penny's desire to own us made the decision easy.

*Bear* with me as I call attention to the way we use animal names in similes and as a means of brightening expressions. I'm not merely *hogtied*, I have *butterflies in my stomach*, for I know I'll miss many—make that most—of the fur people that come to your mind. Therefore, I don't promise a rundown of all the bizarre and wonderful creatures that crawl, fly or walk on this earth.

Shall we start with the word *ant*? We often say we're *antsy*. Some might even say they *have ants in the pants*.

Then there is the word *ape*. We use *ape* to mean we copy something or somebody. We also *go ape* over something we like.

We say someone has *bats in the belfry*.

We say *he's a bear today*. Better still, we talk about *bear hugs*. They're nice to give and wonderful to receive.

We often mention *bees* as *bees' knees*, *beeline*, or *busy as a bee*.

We say a *bird in the hand is worth two in the bush*. We say *birds of a feather flock together*. And we refer to *bird legs*.

If you won't *bug me* I'll go on to talk about someone who is *strong as a bull*, or who *takes the bull by the horns*.

Next we have some of my favorites. We have *nervous as a long-tailed cat in a room full of rocking chairs*, *cat's meow*, *cat's-paw*, *cat's whiskers*, *catnap*, *hepcat* and *cat's pajamas*. And, if we're not careful, we'll *let the cat out of the bag*, or look *like the cat that swallowed the canary*, or *like something the cat dragged in*. A *dead-cat bounce* is in reference to stock market activity. The *cat's got my tongue*, but there's no need to *pussyfoot* around about it.

To say we're *chicken* means that we're cowardly. A job seeker said he was *chicken* to go in that door. He was told to get moving and not to *wait 'til the cows come home* if he wanted a job. He was *happy as a clam* when he landed one. However, his first paycheck was just *chicken feed*.

Often when we refer to the *crow* we talk about *crow's feet* around the eyes. We say we have *something to crow about*, *as the crow flies*, and we say we *have to eat crow*. Ugh. And surely sailors won't let us forget the *crow's nest*, a platform on a mast.

You *lucky dog*! Now we get to talk about those lovely loyal canines. Let's hope you're not *leading a dog's life*, *in the dog house*, experiencing *dog-eat-dog*, needing *the hair of the dog that bit you*, *sick as a dog*, an *underdog*, nor *dog tired*. Surely, you're not *nuthin' but a hound dog*. Let's also hope it's not *raining cats and dogs* where you are. If so, it would be tough to *put on the dog*. There's more about dogs. We talk about *dog tags*, *dog in the manger*, *dog days* and *dog years*, that *dog won't hunt*, when

*Hector was a pup, letting sleeping dogs lie, every dog has his day, dog-ear, puppy love,* and the Brits even say *dogsbody* for a simple servant, a drudge or subordinate.

Golfers are wary of the *dogleg*, the golf hole in which the fairway is abruptly angled.

Those in the navy are too fully aware of the *dogwatch*, a reference to either of two periods of watch duty, from 4 to 6 p.m. or 6 to 8 p.m. *Dogwatch* also refers to a late night shift.

I won't *duck* my duty on this one. Nor will I do a *duck walk*, and I refuse to be an *ugly duckling*, or a *lame duck*.

Do you ever wonder why an unwanted something is called a *white elephant*? Maybe if you had the *memory of an elephant* you could remember why. And, let's not forget the elephant and the donkey as political symbols.

Do you ever feel *like a fish out of water*?

Or believe you were *outfoxed*?

I've already told you about the *frog in my throat*, so I'll *leapfrog* to the next item on our list.

Does all this give you *goose bumps*? Or does it make you feel *silly as a goose* for reading all this?

My Dad was fond of saying I was *knee-high to a grasshopper*, so all this has gone on for a *coon's age*.

While we're here with the letter G, let's salute the after-dinner drink named for the *grasshopper*. It consists of Creme de Menthe, Creme de Cacoa and cream and is delicious the way they make it at Sorrento's restaurant.

The *groundhog*, a short-legged animal with grizzly brown fur, has its own special day. Every year on the second of February you'll hear about and read about the groundhog. And, the greeting card industry will sell you a card commemorating the day. One certainly has to admire the P.R. person who created the legend of Punxsutawney Phil. Punxsutawney Phil is the most famous denizen of Punxsutawney, Pennsylvania. Phil is a groundhog with a mission. He takes center stage at Gobbler's Knob on Groundhog Day, in the early morning. He is placed in a heated burrow beneath a simulated tree stump on the stage. There he waits till 7:45 a.m., when he is brought out to make his prediction. All eyes focus on him as a great gathering of folks from all over await the outcome. He is checking the weather. If it is sunny and he sees his shadow, he expects storms will come and retreats inside to hibernate for six more weeks of winter. If it is overcast and he does not see his shadow, he expects moderate weather and remains above ground as spring is near.

A good quote about a hen is *as scarce as hen's teeth*. Maybe one should visit a *hen party* to learn more about it. No need to be *mad as a wet hen*.

*Hold your horses* for I want to talk about getting *on one's high horse* to deliver something *straight from the horse's mouth*. I don't like a *dark horse, horse play, a horse laugh, beating a dead horse*, nor attempting to *lead a horse to water*. But then, all that would be a *horse of a different color*.

Oscar Wilde had a great definition of *horse sense*. He maintained that "Horse sense is what keeps horses from betting on what people will do."

A *laughing hyena* comes in here.

We've all heard about a *kangaroo court* and probably thought the Aussies coined the phrase. Not true. The phrase merely refers to any court whose verdict is arranged in advance.

For the letter L we have someone who is *meek as a lamb*, that is, a mild-mannered person. Also for the letter L, we have one who is *happy as a lark*. Next we learn that *a leopard can't change his spots* and that one can be *crazy as a loon*.

Most of us think of a *lion's share* as being most of it. Not so. Lions don't share. The *lion's share* means all of it. And we surely don't wish to *beard the lion in his den*.

I don't want to *monkey around* in my *monkey suit*, and I don't want *a monkey on my back*. I'd feel like a *monkey's uncle* if I did. So I guess you won't *make a monkey* of me. Surely you're not up to those mischievous pranks we call *monkeyshines*.

We have a couple of references to mouse. We can be *quiet as a mouse*. And, of course, we have the computer *mouse*. We can also use the word *mouse* to refer to that discolored swelling under the eye. Perhaps when someone responded to our being *stubborn as a mule*.

Don't you wish you were *wise as an owl*?

The letter P makes us think of pigs. We have a *pig in a poke*. We are told *you can't make a silk purse out of a sow's ear*. We have *when pigs fly*. Pigs certainly fly in Cincinnati every year when there is a Flying Pig Marathon. And we must not forget the *guinea pig*, that small, short-eared domesticated rodent. The informal meaning of *guinea pig* refers to a person who is used as an object for experimentation or research.

According to Woody Allen, *pigeons are rats with wings*. And, how about *stool pigeon*, and *pigeonhole*?

We're sometimes as *prickly as a porcupine*.

We *play possum*.

Here's one I didn't expect. I thought I enjoyed *Welsh rarebit*. Turns out it's *Welsh rabbit*. I learned this from Evan Morris, the word detective, who says the dish is rabbit, as in the hopping critter with the big ears.

All of us get ourselves into a *rat race* at times. Here's hoping we don't meet the kind of rat that betrays comrades or deserts his ship.

Let's hope you never meet a *shark*. Not even a *loan shark*.

If you see a youngster with a *sheepish grin*, you can bet the child is up to no good.

For snakes we have *snake in the grass* and *snake eyes*.

Did you *squirrel away* your candy when you were a child?

For tiger, there is *tiger by the tail* and *Tiger Rag*. There is also a *paper tiger*. As you know, the paper tiger appears to be as strong as the real tiger but is actually weak.

Turtles seem to evoke thoughts of *turtle doves*. And, how about *turn turtle*?

We talk about *a wolf in sheep's clothing*, and worse still, being *fed to the wolves*.

*Zebras* come in all shapes and stripes, especially those officiating at football and basketball games.

For more than thirty-eight years the animals on TV's Sesame Street have beguiled viewers young and old. It's worth an hour or two of your time to visit there.

Also, take more than a cursory glance at the way advertisers employ animals to send their messages.

Surely you don't think that AFLAC is using a silly goose to impart its message. More like the "golden goose." Don't you agree?

I'm a bit embarrassed to tell you this, but one of my most successful talks—in terms of audience acceptance—got off to a great start because I came to the podium dressed as the Energizer Bunny. Serendipity was at work here. One: I'd won a prize on a cruise ship with the costume. Two: when asked to return for what must have been my fourth or fifth talk before the National Human Resources Association, they kindly answered my "No go" with, as far as they were concerned I was "going strong," and could "keep on going and going." How could I resist? After all, this provided the chance to use a new gimmick.

Suzanne Packard, fitness guru, knows how effective animal imagery can be and proves it with the help of stuffed animals. And Suzanne is particularly fetching in her reindeer get-up. Those bobbing antlers do keep class participants attentive.

If you think all this animal talk has no merit, consider how the creators of comic strips get help from animals; for example, there are Snoopy, Marmaduke, Garfield, Opus and many others. Then there's TV's Mr. Ed. Could the Biblical reference to a talking donkey have inspired Mr. Ed's writers? For the Biblical account, check Second Peter 2:16 for the reference to Balaam, "A dumb ass spoke with human voice and restrained the prophet's madness."

# SMALL TALK

Out of the Mouths of Babes

This segment is not for you who agree with W. C. Fields' assessment of children, i.e., "They shouldn't be seen, let alone be heard." This offering is for you who responded favorably to Art Linkletter's appreciation of some of the darndest things children say.

Admittedly, I hoped to provide a chortle or two for you with these sayings from children. However, when you look at the world through the eyes of a child, you often latch onto a nugget you've mined from their sayings. Such nuggets can serve to brighten whatever comes out of your mouth.

"Children are a great comfort in your old age—and they help you reach it faster, too."—Lionel M. Kaufman

Following Art Linkletter's practice of savoring some of those "darndest things," I've acquired a virtual "mother lode" of priceless gems from fertile little brains.

I still chuckle when I ponder the parental reaction when their little one told them the Sunday School lesson was all about, "You'll get your blanket." The teacher had assured her class, "Your comforter cometh."

In another Sunday School class the teacher explained to the youngsters that "Christmas is Christ's birthday." "How old is he gonna' be?" one of them asked.

Then there was the kindergartner who reported that her teacher threatened to "drop her into the furnace for being bad." Not so. The teacher merely told the child she'd be "dropped from the register" if she didn't behave.

I was delighted when the Duccillis, parents of my friend Emilie, invited my small son and me to dinner. I was not delighted when he stopped all conversation with this announcement: "My Mother's going to marry Bruce Martin but he doesn't know it yet." What "little big mouth" didn't add was that he'd eavesdropped when Bruce told me he planned to propose. Good mother that I am, I had discussed with the child the probability of saying "yes" when the proposal came. I tried to explain all this to my hosts, but I couldn't be heard above the laughter.

Shortly after my marriage to Bruce, a widower, my son learned that he would gain two new grandmothers, my husband's mother and the mother of his late wife. Members of the family were pleased and amused when the boy blurted out, "A kid can't have too many grandmas." Smart boy, my son.

Always a Bil Keane fan for his *The Family Circus*, I see that I've saved a couple of his cartoons. In one, the tiny son asks if his father was born before the "Silver War." In another, the tiny daughter reports that she wished Mrs. Goldman "a Happy Harmonica."

Sometimes the "funny papers" **are** funny. I still enjoy the frame in which "Dennis the Menace" tells his friend Joey that his Dad says this "freezin' cold weather comes from the wind chill factory."

Juliana (I wish I'd recorded her last name) sent me a note about the youngster whose favorite foods are hangburgers and strangled eggs. Thanks Juliana.

Another note reports that a two-year-old who had to spend time in a playpen said, "Get me out of this cage."

I don't know whether to remark on this little girl's creativity or her confidence. She decided to draw a picture of God. Her father said, "Oh honey, nobody knows what God looks like." Little girl: "They will when I get finished."

Connor Laney, at the age of three, looked up at his grandfather Martin and said, "See this hand—no Coke in it."

Tiny Richard sobbed as he asked for a "Bang-aid" for his bruised knee.

Picture, if you will, a huge family reunion where my little cousin Kate made this announcement regarding her brother and a young woman he was dating at the time: "Paul and Peggy are in the living room making a baby." Immediately there was righteous indignation on the part of my Aunt Kathryn. Too late, my mother put her hands over my tiny ears. My cousin Paul, who was unceremoniously brought before his elders, swore innocence. And, a sobbing Peggy could scarcely speak. Later, much later, the grown-ups learned that little Kate hadn't gotten the full "birds and bees" story. She thought kissing was the way you made babies.

How's this for stress? I was baby sitting my baby son and small nephew at the home of my parents-in-law. Because their door seemed to lock automatically, I cautioned my nephew to "never, never touch that lock." Shortly before lunch, I took Johnny and the baby out to the side garden. You guessed it. When I tried to go inside, the door was securely locked. Because I had cookies in the oven and clothes in the dryer, I had to borrow a neighbor's car to go in search of my parents-in-law at the mall. What I was shouting to Johnny I can't remember, but I do know I had to pull over to the side of the road as Johnny whimpered, "I sure hope Jesus doesn't decide to knock my block off for this."

Now we have a couple of excerpts from camp letters: From Jay: "They said I had to write to you or I couldn't eat." And, from nine-year-old Shirlie, we have a postscript from her camp letter, "A snake I was playing with yesterday bit me." Presumably Shirlie was okay by the time the letter arrived.

I've been saving these Kateisms from her mother Dr. Terri Byczkowski for a long time. Kate referred to this morning, yesterday and tomorrow as follows: "The morning before this night, the day before this day, and the day after this day." Makes sense to me.

Kate and her mother also had this conversational exchange. Kate: "I didn't sleep last night." Mother: "You sure did, you were sound asleep." Kate: "I was not. I was sleeping wide awake all night." When Kate woke up with a hoarse voice, she said, "Mom, my voice is gone."

Here's some choice word mangling I saved from a column Ginny Hunter wrote for *The Cincinnati Post*. She reported that little Amy referred to the Eiffel Tower as the "Rifle Tower." After a devastating tornado Amy worried that another tomato would come. In the first grade Amy worked on a class project with destruction paper. In the second grade, she memorized the Apostles Creek. As she grew a little older she learned to sing *Taps* in the Girl Scouts. She sang, "From the lakes, from the hills, from the sky, All is well, safely rest, God is nice" (nigh).

Here's more from a little boy I know: He referred to "Custard's last stand." He wanted to ride the "alligator" (escalator) at Macy's, and he thought it unfair that he couldn't go to Zoo Day because he had "chicken pops" (pox). Now for two more: On seeing a stopped train, he remarked, "Me thinks it ran out of batteries." And, on seeing lightning, the same small boy ran to the door and cried, "Oh take my picture, take my picture."

Four-year-old Jacob remarked upon seeing twins, "I never saw any two of 'ems before." His sister also had a great comment about babies. She hoped a very pregnant relative would have a boy because as she put it, "I don't want to be an aunt."

Little Jeanne Yarborough upon approaching her fourth birthday announced, "I'll be four in the next minute." She also when told that Daddy was too busy driving to watch for dogs exclaimed, "Daddy you watch for dogs, I'll drive." Little Jeanne also liked "zoo cookies" (animal crackers).

Another Amy, this one at the age of ten, took gymnastics after school. She promised to stay in shape "until I'm thirty-nine." After that, she said, "I'll be too old."

Mark Patinkin amused me with a piece he wrote for the Scripps-Howard News Service. Mark said that for years he used to catch butterflies in the *bacon* lot at the corner of his block. Until he was ten he was convinced that strips of bacon were growing beneath the underbrush.

The woman Mark married, Heidi, told him she had a hard time as a child when she had to sing a certain hymn about "bringing in the sheets."

Little Brett Foster had a good way of expressing the word everybody. Brett said, "All bodies."

I'm not sure where or when I stashed this one but I love it. Upon finding one of her students making faces at others, a teacher gently reproved the child. Smiling sweetly, the teacher said, "When I was a child, I was told if I made ugly faces, my face would freeze like that." The student looked up and replied, "Well, you can't say you weren't warned."

Here's another from my files. A three-year-old says to his grandmother, "Grandma, I'm hungry." Grandma: "You're hungry?" Grandson: "Yes, can't you feel my belly growling?"

Attorney and author Bill Whalen tells this on Jillian, his granddaughter, who was three. She reported that "Mom and Dad are old, but Grandpa is real old." One day when Jillian and her mother Kelly were both upset, Jillian turned to her mother and said, "I don't like your attitude." With a vocabulary such as that at age three, it would seem that Jillian has the makings of an attorney. Don't you agree?

I enjoyed reading about the young daughter of veteran meteorologist Veronica Johnson of WRC-TV in Washington. The little girl said, "Mommy, I told you I didn't like thunderstorms, but you keep making it thunder."

Please tell me you haven't already heard this one about the little girl from Connecticut who recited the Lord's prayer in this manner, "Our father who art in New Haven, how did you know my name?" Another small girl learning the Lord's prayer was heard to recite, "Thy kingdom come, I'll be undone…"

Five-year-old Jenny thought those from Vermont were Vermonsters. Wonder what she would call those from Paris. Parasites?

I believe it's only fair that I close this segment with one of my own word manglings. It seems that my parents so enjoyed my referring to deviled eggs as "devilish eggs" that they encouraged the mistake until the day our minister was due to have lunch with us. I became upset and told Mother, "The minister will punish us if we try to give him devilish eggs."

# PART VI

Words of Farewell

# WORDS OF FAREWELL

### Julius Caesar

Probably the most famous words of farewell were these from Julius Caesar to Marcus Junius Brutus, "Et tu brute."

On March 15 (the Ides of March) in 44 B.C. Marcus Junius Brutus and Gaiu Cassius led a group of aristocrats in a plot to kill Caesar. They stabbed him to death as he entered a senate meeting. He received more than 20 wounds from men who had accepted his favors. Small wonder that Caesar's statement as he died at the hands of his friends (especially Brutus) remains a leading example of never-to-be-forgotten words of betrayal.

### George Washington (1732-1799) 1st President of the United Sates

Words spoken about Washington after his death remain in our memory even more vividly than the words of Washington himself. Did you have to memorize this from the eulogy spoken by Washington's friend Henry Lee? They were, "He was the first in war, first in peace and first in the hearts of his countrymen." Washington's words of farewell were, "I am about to die and I am not afraid to die. I thank you for your attention and I pray you to take no more trouble for me. Let me go quietly. I cannot last long."

### James Madison (1751-1836) 4th President of the United Sates

Madison's dying words were, "I always think better lying down."

His vivacious wife Dolley, more outgoing and popular than her husband, served as the official White House hostess for both Madison and Jefferson. Dolley was noted for her bravery as well as for her wit and beauty. She saved George Washington's portrait from the burning capital during the War of 1812.

### Abraham Lincoln (1809-1865) 16th President of the United States

Lincoln was renowned as a storyteller and writer. We had to study so many of his words and even some of those in the volumes written about him. Yet few of us remember the parting words of Lincoln's assassin, John Wilkes Booth, "Tell my mother I died for my country. I thought I did it (the assassination) for the best," he said.

### Ulysses Simpson Grant (1822-1885) 18th President of the United States

Grant's final word was a request for "water" as he lay dying of cancer. He died at Mount McGregor near Saratoga, New York, on July 23, 1885. His body now lies in a great tomb on Riverside Drive in New York City. The tomb was paid for by popular subscription, and was dedicated in 1897.

Doubtless those of you who listened to Groucho Marx know some of this for Groucho's favorite question was, "Who is buried in Grants' tomb?"

Grant wrote two volumes that were published by the noted author, Mark Twain. Grant died without knowing what success his memoirs were to achieve, but his family received nearly a half-million dollars from the volumes.

### James A. Garfield (1831-1881) 20th President of the United States

The final words spoken at the assassination of President Garfield were those of his assassin, Charles J. Guiteau. After shooting President Garfield in the back, Guiteau said, "I am a stalwart and Arthur is president now."

### William McKinley (1843-1901) 25th President of the United States

As many who read history know, President McKinley was killed by an anarchist named Leon Czolgosz. Leon Czolgosz joined a group of people who were in line to shake hands with the President while they were at a public reception held in the Temple of Music at the Pan-American Exposition in Buffalo. Czolgosz came forward to meet McKinley with a revolver hidden in a bandage around his right hand. As he drew near, he fired, and a bullet penetrated the President's stomach.

History buffs also know that President McKinley was extremely devoted to his wife Ida. Ida McKinley was frail and in precarious health, and McKinley was always very protective of her. As he lay mortally wounded his thoughts were of Ida. He implored his secretary, "Be careful how you tell her—oh, be careful."

**Warren Gamaliel Harding** (1861-1929) 29th President of the United States

President Harding died as his wife, Florence Harding, read to him. He seemed to appreciate one of the few favorable articles written about him (*Saturday Evening Post*) and urged Mrs. Harding to continue, saying, "That's good. Go on, read some more."

**Franklin Delano Roosevelt** (1882-1045) 32nd President of the United States

Roosevelt was the only President to be elected to office four times. He made many speeches (the "fireside chats" during World War II were widely heard and widely quoted). His last words were these: "I have a terrific headache." He died soon after of a cerebral hemorrhage.

**Dwight David Eisenhower** (1890-1969) 34th President of the United States

President Eisenhower was ready to die after numerous heart attacks and congestive heart failure. He is reputed to have said, "I want to go—God take me." He died in 1969 at the age of 79.

When Eisenhower retired to his farm in Pennsylvania he devoted much of his time to his memoirs. In 1963 he published "Mandate for Change," which was followed in 1965 by "Waging Peace." A lighter work, "At Ease: Stories I Tell to Friends," appeared in 1967.

In both presidential campaigns his opponent was Adlai Stevenson. In 1952 Stevenson won more votes than any previous losing candidate in history. Stevenson was known for his wit, his speaking ability, and the high literacy of his speeches. Aware of the power of words, Stevenson said that Eisenhower won the presidency only because his campaign manager coined "that odious phrase, I like Ike." Stevenson also said he regretted that he was too much of a gentleman to tell the nation's cat lovers that "Ike abhorred cats."

### Lou Gehrig, byname of Henry Louis Gehrig

From June 1, 1925 to May 2, 1939, the "Iron Horse" played first base for the New York Yankees. He left baseball with the record of a career batting average of .340, 493 homers, and 1990 runs batted in. He also left mesmerized fans with an always-to-be-remembered farewell speech called "Baseball's Gettysburg Address."

In his farewell speech at Yankee Stadium in 1939, he said, "Fans, for the past two weeks you have been reading about the bad break I got. Yet today I consider myself the luckiest man on the face of the earth." Lou referred to the diagnosis of amylotrophic lateral sclerosis, often called ALS, as his bad break. After Lou's death, the disease would bear his name—"Lou Gehrig Disease."

After that opening statement, Lou went on to praise his wife, his parents, his mother-in-law, his teammates, his manager, and even the groundskeeper. He closed by saying, "I may have had a bad break, but I've got an awful lot to live for."

### Cal Ripken, Jr.

Cal Ripken, Jr., called baseball's "Everyman in Spikes," was a player who made his name less for his greatness with bat and glove than for coming to work every day.

In his "Farewell to Baseball Address" he said: "As a kid, I had this dream. Tonight, we close a chapter of this dream—my playing career. My dreams for the future include pursuing my passion for baseball. Hopefully, I will be able to share what I have learned. And, I would be happy if that sharing would lead to something as simple as a smile on the face of others. I might also add that if, if I am remembered, I hope it's because, by living my dream, I was able to make a difference. Thank you.

### Conrad Hilton

Conrad Hilton, who was called "the biggest hotel man in the world," was asked if he had any final words for the American people. "Yes," he said, "Leave the shower curtain on the inside of the tub."

### Major General John Sedgwick

According to the inscription on the monument honoring him at Spotsylvania, Virginia, General Sedgwick arrived there on the morning of May 9, 1864 to direct some minor redeployment of his troops. Ignoring warnings from his chief-of-staff, Sedgwick stalked about admonishing his men to cease worrying about the occasional fire of Confederate sharpshooters concealed in the woodline far to their front. "I am ashamed of you, dodging that way," scolded Sedgwick. "They couldn't hit an elephant at this distance."

Shortly thereafter, a bullet slammed into the general's face, killing him almost instantly. The shot came from a Whitworth rifle at a distance of more than 500 yards.

Popular lore has improved the story by saying his final statement was, "They couldn't hit an elephant at this dist…"

### Alexander Hamilton

In 1804, Alexander Hamilton, brilliant statesman and first Secretary of the United States Treasury, became involved in a political dispute with Aaron Burr, then Vice President. The two men were old rivals in New York politics and in law practice. Burr challenged Hamilton to a duel, in which Hamilton was killed.

Hamilton's last words were these: "This is a mortal wound. Take care of that pistol. It is undischarged and still cocked. It might go off and do harm. I did not intend to fire at him."

### Ludwig van Beethoven

One of the most poignant farewell messages is that of Beethoven. Afflicted with deafness, this awesomely talented composer said as he lay dying of pneumonia, "I shall hear in heaven."

### Thomas Edison

Like Beethoven, Thomas Edison suffered from hearing loss. As he lay dying he looked out his bedroom window and said these final words, "It's very beautiful over there."

### The Reverend Martin Luther King, Jr.

"I've looked over. And I have seen the promised land." The Reverend Martin Luther King, Jr. spoke those words to a Memphis audience the night before he as assassinated.

The civil rights leader, self-named "Drum Major for Justice," motivated many followers to seek a promised land where freedom, justice and equality reign supreme.

### 0. Henry, byname of William Sydney Porter

The famous satirist uttered these words as he died, "Turn up the lights. I don't want to go home in the dark."

### Geronimo (Geronimo was the name given him by the Mexicans. His real Apache name was Goyahkla—"One Who Yawns.")

Upon his surrender to General George Cook, Geronimo said, "Once I moved about like the wind. Now I surrender to you and that is all."

### George Gipp, known as The Gipper

"Win one for the Gipper." University of Notre Dame's legendary coach Knute Rockne said he made that plea to fulfill a promise he'd made to George Gipp when Gipp was on his death bed.

Gipp had entered Notre Dame on a baseball scholarship, but Rockne recruited him for football when he saw him drop-kicking and passing a football on a field adjacent to the practice field. In one game Gipp was apparently going to punt but instead drop-kicked a 62-yard field goal. In his last season Gipp played injured and a persistent cold developed into pneumonia, leading to his death.

At halftime during a scoreless game versus Army, Rockne challenged his team with that famous statement. Notre Dame won.

### Jim Valvano

Jim Valvano, the beloved basketball coach of North Carolina State, made a long farewell speech called "The Courage Award Address." His opening words were, "Thank you, thank you very much. Thank you." The applause must have been deafening at that point.

Valvano closed his talk with these words: "I know, I gotta go, I gotta go, and I got one last thing and I said it before, and I'm gonna say it again: Cancer can take away all my physical ability. It cannot touch my mind; it cannot touch my heart; and it cannot touch my soul. And those three things are going to carry on forever. I thank you and God bless you all."

## Tennyson

Few have expressed words of farewell so beautifully as the poet Alfred Lord Tennyson in his poem, "Crossing the Bar."

> Sunset and evening star,
>
> And one clear call for me!
>
> And may there be no moaning of the bar,
>
> When I put out to sea.
>
> But such a tide as moving seems asleep,
>
> Too full for sound and foam,
>
> When that which drew me out the boundless deep
>
> Turns again home.
>
> Twilight and evening bell,
>
> And after that the dark!
>
> And may there be no sadness of farewell,
>
> When I embark;
>
> For tho' from out our bourne of Time and Place
>
> The flood may bear me far,
>
> I hope to see my Pilot face to face
>
> When I have crossed the bar.

## Mel Blanc

The voice that delighted so many of us when we watched cartoons was often that of Mel Blanc. Remember Porky Pig and all those great cartoon characters who would sign off with "Th-a-t-s all folks?" Those famous words served as Mel Blanc's epitaph.

## The Deathbed Statement

Let's pause for a moment here to mention the deathbed statement. Under normal conditions, no person may testify in court as to what any person other than the defendant said to him or in his hearing. The one exception is the deathbed statement, and the rules that define it are rather specific. The conditions are: The person making the deathbed statement must know that he of she is dying and then actually die.

# THE LAST WORD

The last word is yours. Please use it to tell me about words that nourish your psyche, also about words or phrases you'd like to expunge from our language.

Send to:     Phyllis Martin

jmartin660@cinci.rr.com

Lake Superior State University welcomes your nominations for the Banished Words List. Word-watchers pull nominations throughout the year from everyday speech, as well as from the news, fields of education, technology, advertising, politics, and more. A committee gathers the entries and chooses the best in December. The list is released on New Year's Day. LSSU has been compiling the lists since 1976, choosing from nominations sent from around the world.

Lake Superior State University accepts nominations for the List of Banished Words throughout the year. To submit your nominations for the next list, go to www.lssu.edu/banished.

Lake Superior State University is located at 650 W. Easterday Ave., Sault Ste. Marie, Ml 449783. Their phone number is (906) 632-6841.

A list of the 100 most often mispronounced words and phrases can be found at: http://www.yourdictionary.com/library/mispron.html

# BIBLIOGRAPHY

*Crazy English* by Richard Lederer, Published by Pocket Books 1990

*Death Sentences* by Don Watson, Published by Gotham Books 2005

*Eats, Shoots & Leaves* by Lynne Truss, Published by Gotham Books 2004

*Famous Last Words*, Compiled by Ray Robinson, Printed by Workman Publishing, 2003

*The Game of Words* by William R. Espy, Published by Branhall House 1972

The Holy Bible

*How to Be the Life of the Podium* by Sylvia Simmons, Published by amacom 1991

*Lapsing Into a Comma*, by Bill Walsh, Published by Contemporary Books 2000

*The Logophile's Orgy* by Lewis Burke Frumkes, Published by Delacorte Press 1995

*The New Dictionary of Thoughts*, Published by the Standard Book Company 1956

*Oxford Dictionary of Quotations*—Second Edition, Published by Oxford University Press 1955

*A Pleasure in Words* by Eugene T. Maleska, Published by Simon and Schuster 1981

*The Right Word in the Right Place at the Right Time* by William Safire, published by Simon & Schuster 2004

*Scene of the Crime,* by Anne Wingate, Ph.D., Published by Writer's Digest Books 1992

*The Word Detective* by Evan Morris, Published by Algonquin Books 2000

*Word Watcher's Handbook, A Deletionary of the Most Abused and Misused Words* by Phyllis Martin, an Author's Guild Backinprint Book 2000. Third Edition by St. Martin's Press 1991

Phyllis Martin is a former employment counselor for The Procter & Gamble Company and career columnist for *The Cincinnati Post*. Her articles have appeared in *Newsday, Cosmopolitan, Writer's Digest, Moneypaper, Working Woman,* and *The New York Times Syndicate*.

Her nine books have sold more than 250,000 copies.

According to her, the greatest achievement is the selling of thirteen of her poems. And you thought rhyme didn't pay. (Admittedly, not much).

She presents two word vignettes each week for public radio's WMKV-FM and is the business writer for *Altro Telescope*, a webzine.

# INDEX

abbreviations (states), 15, 35-38
Abd-el-Kader, 5
accept/except, 28
accidentally, 28
adverse/averse, 20
advice, 41-42
affect/effect, 28
affidavid, 20-21
aggravate, 29
Allen, Fred, 44
Allen, Woody, 12, 68
alot, 18
already/all ready, 29
alright, 29
America, 42
among, 29, 45
Ampère, A.M., 53
Amy, 73-74
Andersen, Hans Christian, 47
Angelou, Maya, 44, 46
anger, 42
angry at/angry with, 29
anniversary, 21, 23
ant, 65
anxious, 29
anyplace, 29
anywhere, 18, 29
ape, 65

appearance, 9
Aristotle, 42, 45, 61
Arthur, President Chester A., 80
ass, 69
Association for Women in Communications, 4
at, 29
athlete, 29
author, 4, 29
ax, 29

Balaam, 69
Ballou, Hosea, 42
Barrie, James A., 47
Baruch, Barnard M., 49
bats, 65
bear, 61, 64-65
bees, 65
Beethoven, Ludwig van, 83
Begon, Michel, 53
Belasco, David, 48
Benefits, 12
Bentley, E. Clerihew, 55
between you and I, 18, 29
Bierce, Ambrose, 48
bird, 65
birds and bees, 72
Blanc, Mel, 86

Blasingame, Jim, 11
Bloomer, Amelia, 53
Blurb, Belinda, 54
bones, 12
Book of Revelation, 21-22, 47
Booth, John Wilkes, 80
boughten, 29
Boycott, Charles C., 54
brainstorming, 9
Bremer, Frederika, 5
brevity, 4
Brinkley, David, 12
British, 23, 42, 66
Brutus, Marcus Junius, 79
bug, 65
bull, 65
Bulwer-Lytton, Edward, 4, 46
bumper sticker, 42
bunny, 69
Burgess, Gelett, 54
Burnside, Ambrose, 60
Burr, Aaron, 83
Bushnell, Horace, 45
busy, 9, 65
Butler, Rhett, 45
Butler, Samuel, 47
butterflies, 64, 74
Byczkowski, Kate, 73
Byczkowski, Terri, v, 73
Byron, 5, 9

Caesar, Julius, 79
Calvary/cavalry, 30
can't hardly, 18, 30

Cardigan, Earl of, 54
carve/chiseling, 9
Cassius, Gaiu, 79
cat, 48, 64-65, 81
Cato, 49
chance, 11, 22
change, 4, 9, 81
Charrier, Marian, v, ix
chasm, 30
Chaucer, 49
Chauvin, Nicolas, 55
Chesterfield, Earl of, 55
Cheyfitz, Kirk, 25
chicken, 65
childish/childlike, 30
children, 34, 47, 70-75
*Cincinnati Post*, 4, 73
Cincinnati Reds, 26
citizen, 21
clam, 65
clerihew, 55
clichés, 24-26
Clinton, President William, 53, 55
Cobb, Bob, 55
Collins, John Charlton, 41
Colton, Caleb C., 4
commonwealth, 23
complected, 30
confidence, 9, 72
congratulations, 21, 23
consultant, 9
contacts, 11
contents, vii
conversation, 6, 19-20

conversational pie, 15, 18-20
Cook, General George, 84
coon's age, 66
courage, 42
cow, 54
creativity, 9, 72
credible/credulous, 30
credit, 30, 42
creditable, 30
criticism, 42
Cronkite, Walter, 31
crow, 65
Czolgosz, Leon, 80

Daguerre, Louis J.M., 55
Dahl, Anders, 55
data, 23, 30
Davenport, 55
death, dying, 43, 79-85
deathbed statement, 86
December, 30
Deen, Paula, 47
Dennis the Menace, 71
Derrick, Thomas, 55
Derringer, Henry, 55
de Sade, Comte Donatien, 60
Diehl, Pat, v
Diesel, Rudolph, 56
discrete/discreet, 21-22
dog, 65-66
donkey, 66, 69
Doyly, 56
Draco, 56
Duccilli, Emilie, 71

duck, 66
dunce, 56
Dunne, Finley Porter, 42
Duplessis-Pralin, Marshal, 59

Ebb, Fred, 46
Edison, Thomas A., 10, 83
education, 3, 11, 43-44, 46, 87
Edwards, Tryon, 43
ego, 41
Eisenhower, President Dwight David, 81
elder/older, 30
elephant, 66, 83
Eliot, George, 50
Elvis, 45
Emerson, Ralph Waldo, 4, 10
enthused, 30
envy, 43, 50
epitaph, 43, 86
eponyms, 51, 53-62
escape, 30
Eschenlohr, Wolf, v
espresso, 30
Essex, Earl of, 55
et cetera, 30
Eveleigh, Phyllis, 42
experiment, 30

Fahrenheit, Gabriel, 42
failure, 10, 12, 47
faith, 46, 62
fame, 10
famed, 30

famous people, 44
farther/further, 31
fashion, 44
fear, 42, 45
February, 31
fewer/less, 31
fictional characters, 45
Fields, W.C., 44, 70
fiscal/physical, 31
fish, 66
folly, 45
for free, 31
Ford, Henry, 10
Ford, President Gerald R., 3
forgiveness, 45
Forsyth, William, 56
forte, 21, 23
fortuitous, 21-22
Fosdick, Harry Emerson, 46
Foster, Brett, 74
Fowler, H.W., 22
fox, 66
France, Anatole, 11
friends, 10, 79
frog, 66
Fuchs, Leonard, 56
future, 10

Galvani, Luigi, 56
Garden, Dr. Alexander, 56
Garfield, 69
Garfield, President James A., 80
Gatling, Richard J., 56
Gaudi, Antonio, 56

Gay, John, 43
Gehrig, Lou, 82
Geiger, Hans, 57
Geller, Ronald, 3
genius, 11
Gentius, King of Illyria, 57
Geronimo, 84
Gerry, Eldridge, 57
Gipp, George, 84
Glaser, Marion, v, 26
goals, 11-12
God, 9, 11, 41, 43, 45-47, 72-73, 81, 85
Goethe, 46, 49
Goizueta, Roberto, 11
gold, 3, 5, 10, 59
Goldwyn, Sam, 44
Goodwill, 12
goose, 66, 69
graduate, 46
grammar, 17
Granger, J., 57
Grant, President Ulysses Simpson, 80
grasshopper, 66
Greeley, Horace, 11
Greenfield, Albert M., 11
groom, 23
groundhog, 66-67
Guillotin, Joseph Ignace, 57
guinea pig, 68
Guiteau, Charles J., 80

had of, 31
Hamilton, Alexander, 83
Hamlin, Sonya, 13

Hammer, David, 63
Hancock, John, 44
Hansom, J.A., 57
Harding, Florence, 81
Harding, President Warren Gamaliel, 81
Havelock, Sir Henry, 57
healthful/healthy, 31
hear-ache, 17-18, 20, 31
heartrending, 31
Heidi, 74
heighth, 18
hen, 32, 67
Henry, O., 84
here's two ways to, 31
Hiles, Eileen, v
Hilton, Conrad, 82
Hirtl, Leo, 4
hog, 64
Holmes, Oliver Wendell, 3, 10, 44, 47
Holmes, Sherlock, 45
Hooper, Ben, 45
hope, 46, 62
Horace, 42
horse, 67
Hubbard, E., 41, 43
Hugo, Victor, 50
human resources, 9
humble, 31, 41
humor, 9, 22, 46
Hunter, Ginny, 73
Hutchins, Robert M., 46
hyena, 67

I/me, 18, 29
idea, 11, 48
Ides of March, 79
I don't think, 31
Illinois, 31
imply/infer, 31
incidentally, 32
index, 32, 91
individual, 32
ingenious/ingenuous, 32
in parenthesis, 32
Institution/Institute, 20
Introduction, ix
invite, 32
irregardless, 18
it don't, 18
Italian, 32
it's/its, 32

Jacob, 13, 73
Jacobson, Emilie, v
Jay, 72
Jerome, Jerome Klapka, 9
jewelry, 32
Jillian, 74
Johnny, 72
Johnson, Samuel, 47
Johnson, Veronica, 74
Juliana, 71

Kamel, Georg Josef, 54
kangaroo, 67
Kansas City *Times*, 12
Kaufman, Lionel M., 70

Keane, Bil, 71
Kelly, 74
Kilpatrick, James J., 20, 22, 26
King, Reverend Martin Luther, Jr., 84

Lake Superior State University, 87
lamb, 67
Land, Edwin H., 3
Landers, Ann, 5, 23, 31
Laney, Connor, 72
lark, 67
Lavater, JohnCaspar, 5
lay/lie, 32
learn/teach, 32
leave/let, 32
Lee, Henry, 79
leopard, 61, 67
Leotard, Jules, 58
Levis, 58
Lewis, C.S., 4
library, 33
life, 44, 46-47
like, 33
Lincoln, President Abraham, 80
Linkletter, Art, 70
Linnaeus, Carolus, 57
lion, 67
listening, 18, 20, 41
Logan, James H., 58
long sentences, 4
Long, Professor, 62
Longfellow, 43, 49
loon, 67
Lord's prayer, 74-75

Louis XV, 59
luck, 11, 47
Lynch, James, 58

Macintosh, Charles, 58
Madison, Dolley, 79
Madison, President James, 79
Magdaline, Mary, 58
Magnol, Pierre, 58
manufacture, 33
Marmaduke, 69
marriage, 47, 71
Martin, Bruce, v, 24, 71
Martinet, Jean, 58
Marx, Groucho, 80
Masochism, 58
Mausolus, 58
Maverick, Samuel, 58
Mayo, Will, 44
McAdam, John L., 58
McKinley, Ida, 81
McKinley, President William, 80
meantime/meanwhile, 33
memory, 48
men, 47, 50
Menander, 43
Menken, H.L., 46
Mercer, Camille, v
Mercer, John, 59
Mesmer, Franz Anton, 59
Milton, 43
mischievous, 33
mispronunciation, 31
misused words, 17, 23

Mizner, Wilson, 20, 46
money, 11, 13
monkey, 11, 67
Montaigne, Michel E., 43
Morris, Evan, 68, 90
Moses, 4
most, 33
mouse, 67-68
Mr. Ed, 69
myself, 18

Napoleon I, 59
nauseous/nauseated, 17
nepotism, 11
Neusner, Jacob, 13
Nicot, J., 59
noisome, 33
nuclear, 33

observations, 47
O'Hara, Scarlett, 45
Ohm, G.S., 59
old age, 13, 48-49, 70
once, 33
only, 20, 22
Opus, 69
oral, 33
outdated terms, 26
out loud, 33
Ovid, 43
owl, 68

Packard, Suzanne, 69
partial, 33

Parton, Dolly, 44
Pasteur, Louis, 59
Patinkin, Mark, 74
Patton, General George S., 45
Peel, Sir Robert, 54
pen/sword, 4-5
Penny, 64
persecute/prosecute, 33
persistence, 10-11
persnickety/pernickety, 20-21
personality, 41
personnel, 9
phenomenon, 21, 23
pig, 68
pigeon, 68
Pigg, Rev. Larry H., 49
Pinchbeck, Christopher, 59
podium, 20, 22
Poinsett, J.R., 59
Pompadour, Marquise de, 59
porcupine, 68
Porky Pig, 86
possum, 68
power, 50
praline, 59
prayer, 46
press conference, 21-22
principal/principle, 33
Proctor, Barbara, 11
profanity, 5
professionalism, 5
prone, 34
prophecy/prophesy, 34
prostate/prostrate, 34

Proverbs, 3, 12, 42
Psalms, 6
Pullman, G.M., 59
puns, 44
Punxsutawney Phil, 66

quality, 11
Quisling, Vidkun, 60
quotations, 5

Raglan, Lord, 60
raise/rear, 34
rat, 68
Rath, Millie, v
Reagan, President Ronald, 48
realist, 50
Realtor, 34
recognize, 34
recur, 34
redundancies, 27
regard/regards, 20
regime/regimen, 34
reindeer, 69
relationships, 50
Remington, 12
reputation, 41
retirement, 49
Richter, Jean Paul, 43
Ripkin, Cal, Jr., 82
risk, 11
Ritz, Cesar, 60
Rochefoucauld, duc de La, 6, 45
Rockefeller, John D., Jr., 82
Rockne, Knute, 84

Rogers, Will, 10, 44
Roosevelt, President Franklin Delano, 81
Roosevelt, President Theodore, 47
rut, 10

Sacher-Masoch, 58
sacrilegious, 34
sadistic, 60
Safire, William, 26
sales, 11-12
sanatorium/sanitarium, 34
Sandburg, Carl, 13
Sandwich, Earl of, 60
Santayana, George, 4
savage breast, 5
Sax, Adolphe, 60
Schultz, Charles M., 44
Scott, Walter, 43
Scotus, John Duns, 56
second, 21-22
Sedgwick, Major General John, 83
Seneca, 47
Sequoia, 60
serendipity, 11, 69
sermon, 46, 61
Sesame Street, 69
Shakespeare, William, 5, 41
shark, 12, 68
sheep, 4, 68
sherbet, 34
Shewman, Joyce and Bill, 49
Shirlie, 72
showing up, 12

Shrapnel, General Henry, 60
sideburns, 60
Silhouette, Etienne de, 61
Simonides, 49
Simpson, Julie, 5
Smith, Sydney, 50
snake, 68, 72
Snoopy, 69
somewheres/anywheres, 18
Sophocles, 49
Sorrento's, 66
Spellman, Francis Cardinal, 45
Spooner, Rev. W.A., 61
squirrel, 68
Stamp, Sir Josiah, 43
stateside, 20-21
St. Audrey's fair, 61
Stevenson, Adlai, 81
Strauss, Levi, 58
Strayhorn, Rev. Willie, 62
subject, 13, 43
success, 5, 12, 47
suspicion, 34
swam/swum, 35
Swift, Jonathan, 19
Switzer, Barry, 12

talent, 11, 41
tawdry, 61
temper, 41
temperature, 20-21, 35, 56
tenacity, 13
Tennyson, Alfred Lord, 54, 85
terrible ten, 15, 17-18

that/who, 20, 22
theater, 35
theirselves, 35
Theophrastus, 49
Thomas, Danny, 10
Thoreau, Henry, 4
those kind, 35
tiger, 68
Tillich, Paul, 3
Tillotson, 4
time, 13, 20
Tinervia, Joseph, 32
Tozier, Maureen, 42
training, 13
treachery, 13
turtle, 68
Twain, Mark, 3, 46, 80

unbeknownst, 35
undoubtedly, 35
unique, 35

Valvano, Jim, 84
vanity, 50
Victoria, Queen, 61
Volta, Count Alexander, 61
Voltaire, 46
von Sacher-Masoch, Leopold, 58
von Zeppelin, Count Ferdinand, 62

Walker, Nancy, v
Walpole, Horace, 48
Washington, 35
Washington, President George, 79

Watson, Thomas, 10
Watt, James, 61
ways, 18, 35
Weekley, Ernest, 3
Watson, Thomas, 10
Welsh rabbit/rarebit, 68
West, Mae, 44
Whalen, Bill, 74
White, Mary A., v
Whittier, John Greenleaf, 5
Wilcox, Carlos, 47
Wilde, Oscar, 22, 43, 47, 67
Williams, Grace, 48
Wilson, John, 5
wine, 44
Wistar, Caspar, 61

wolf, 68
woman, 47, 50
Wordsworth, 43
work, 7, 9-13, 45
Wright, Frank Lloyd, 49
writer, 50

Yarborough, Jeanne, 73
you was, 18
Young, Professor, 62
youse, 18

zebra, 68
zeppelin, 62
Ziglar, Zig, 12
Zinn, J.G., 62

978-0-595-38859-2
0-595-38859-0